90

CRASH COURSE

The Life Lessons
My Students Taught Me

KIM BEARDEN

Simon & Schuster

New York   London   Toronto   Sydney   New Delhi

90

Simon & Schuster
1230 Avenue of the Americas
New York, NY 10020

First Simon & Schuster hardcover edition July 2014

SIMON & SCHUSTER and colophon are trademarks of Simon & Schuster, Inc.

For information about special discounts for bulk purchases, please contact Simon & Schuster Special Sales at 1-866-506-1949 or business@simonandschuster.com.

The Simon & Schuster Speakers Bureau can bring authors to your live event. For more information or to book an event, contact the Simon & Schuster Speakers Bureau at 1-866-248-3049 or visit our website at www.simonspeakers.com.

Interior design by Akasha Archer
Jacket design by Tom McKeveny
Jacket photograph by Jeff Amezqua

Manufactured in the United States of America

10 9 8 7 6 5 4 3 2 1

Library of Congress Cataloging-in-Publication Data

Bearden, Kim.
    Crash course : the life lessons my students taught me / Kim Bearden.—
First Simon & Schuster hardcover edition.
        pages cm
1. Teacher-student relationships. 2. Teachers—Conduct of life. I. Title.
LB1033.B41 2014
371.102'3—dc23   2014004693

ISBN 978-1-4516-8770-5
ISBN 978-1-4516-8773-6 (ebook)

To Scotty and Madison,
the two great loves of my life

CONTENTS

CONTENTS

CRASH COURSE

PREFACE

Imagine a one-hundred-year-old, abandoned factory. Dust-caked windows mask sunlight, dilapidated stairwells block passageways, and peeling paint conceals brick walls. Cold air seeps across the muddied floors, punctuated by nails, shattered glass, and forgotten machinery. It is in this place that Ron Clark and I chose to establish the Ron Clark Academy, an innovative middle school in Atlanta of which I am the cofounder, executive director, and language arts teacher.

We discovered the factory after scouring the city for the perfect site. It was an eyesore in the neighborhood and a haven for illicit activity, but somehow we knew that this would be the right spot for us. We had always believed in finding potential in unlikely places. Ron put the proceeds from his first book, *The Essential 55,* into a foundation that we used to purchase the run-down facility. When these monies ran out, committed sponsors came together to support our mission by contributing as well. Three years later, in 2007, our dream became a reality when we opened our doors to our first class of extraordinary students.

PREFACE

Ron Clark and I designed RCA to show how to bring passion, creativity, and rigor into the classroom. We aimed to instill a joy for learning in our students by exposing them to the surrounding world and helping them to understand the importance of giving back to their communities. RCA is also a demonstration school—a place where visiting educators can watch our teachers in action and participate in professional development workshops. In the past seven years, more than 20,000 superintendents, administrators, and teachers from 40 states and 22 countries have visited to observe our classrooms and to learn better ways to engage students, promote academic rigor, and create a climate and culture that promotes student achievement.

We have students of all ability levels at RCA—those who have tested as gifted and those who struggled with failing grades or behavior issues before attending our school. Our students represent varied socioeconomic backgrounds as well. It is our mission to show educators elsewhere that all children have gifts and talents, and when they are put in the hands of dedicated teachers, magic can happen. As a result, our students experience tremendous success. In fact, they have earned millions of dollars in academic scholarships after graduating, and they continue to shine brightly as leaders in their current schools.

Now when you enter RCA, you are greeted by warm hugs and radiant smiles—the spirit of joy is tangible. Vibrant murals and photographs blanket the old brick walls and an electric blue, two-story tube slide fills the lobby and reaches up toward the skylight that spreads sunshine throughout the hallways.

PREFACE

The halls are filled with the sounds of the students' happiness—the music of laughing, singing, hands clapping, and drums beating in celebration. It spills out of lively classrooms, reverberates throughout the corridors, and seeps into the secret passageways of the building.

It is from this tiny old factory that we are creating a revolution in education.

Won't you join us?

COURSE INTRODUCTION

Over the past twenty-seven years, I have served as a teacher, curriculum director, middle school principal, executive director, and school board member. Simultaneously, I have also experienced marriage, motherhood, betrayal, divorce, financial setback, single parenthood, and the joy of finding love and marrying again. Throughout the ups and downs of both my professional and personal life, my students were the light that illuminated my path; they were my sanctuary in the storm.

During these past three decades, I have been blessed to teach over 2,000 students. And each of these children has taught me something about myself, my world, and the abundant capacity for love, resilience, and appreciation that we all possess. When I set out to become an educator, I naively assumed that I would be the one who imparted all of the knowledge; little did I know that the amazing children in my life would teach me more than I could ever hope to learn.

In the pages that follow, I share their stories, for it is their radiance that fills my heart with purpose. My faith has been instrumental in my journey, but this faith has been manifested time and time again through the children around me—my students and my precious daughter. I have seen things through their eyes, and they have inspired me to live passionately and love deeply. In a few instances, some details have been changed to protect the privacy of those involved. But it is my fervent hope that my words adequately capture the essence of their spirits so that you, too, will be forever changed by their brilliance.

1

CHEMISTRY

```
┌─────────────── COURSE DESCRIPTION ───────────────┐
│        In this course, you will learn the importance        │
│                of building relationships.                │
└───────────────────────────────────────────────────┘
```

Freddie was a jolly seventh-grade boy who exploded into my classroom every afternoon at 3:02. His hoarse, booming voice would signal his arrival several moments before he appeared with books, papers, and disheveled articles of clothing swirling around him. Whenever I walked by his desk, I could feel the electricity coming from his body—perhaps this was why his unkempt blond hair always stood on end. Full of one-liners that would go above many of his classmates' heads, Freddie was adept at disrupting the classroom environment and seemed to miss social cues from others. He was the kid who would fall out of his chair for no apparent reason; he was the kid who always seemed to need to go to the bathroom, sharpen his pencil, throw something away, or find any other possible excuse to get out of his seat.

Many teachers and students thought Freddie was highly irritating, and he knew it. He was quick to tell me about their distaste for him, and although he would say it with a chuckle, I could read the sadness behind his bravado. I certainly understood the others' frustrations. Freddie was scheduled into my last-period language arts class every day and he was quite a handful. I could tell within the first five seconds of class whether it would be a good Freddie day or a bad one. However, despite his antics, I knew that there was goodness within him. I saw that Freddie could be clever, creative, and incredibly funny. I embraced his exuberant spirit whenever possible, although I was often required to issue him silent lunches and detentions for misbehavior. Somehow, I just had to teach this kid how to temper his bold personality in order to reach his potential.

One Friday afternoon after my classes, I was called to the front office for an important phone call. I was stunned to discover that I was a finalist for a major teaching award. As I was just trying to process the information being relayed to me, the representative from the Georgia Department of Education explained that seven judges would watch me teach at 3 P.M. on Monday.

My mind began to race. Seven judges? Not a problem. Three o'clock? Huge problem. Three o'clock meant Freddie. So, I did what any logical person would do—I tried to figure out how to get him out of my class. I entertained several scenarios in my mind as I meandered down the long hallway. When I entered my classroom, I sat down to take it all in. Maybe it was a coincidence, but as I reflected, I saw that I was sitting at Freddie's desk. Guilt washed over me. I realized that I would be the world's biggest hypocrite if I tried to create a false sense of nirvana in my classroom just to impress a group of judges.

As I continued to process the situation, I considered what my class must be like from Freddie's perspective. And then I thought about what every day must be like in his world. Freddie must have seen impatience, frustration, and irritation when others looked at him. I wondered if he saw that in my eyes as well.

Over the weekend I struggled to create the perfect lesson plan that would amaze all my guests. But I felt hollow, exhausted, and uninspired. It was a stressful time in my personal life—I was dealing with a broken marriage and my impending divorce, and quite honestly, I just didn't think I had it in me. I wanted to curl into a ball and sleep for a month. Somehow, I found the strength to reevaluate my situation and recommit to my calling to be there for my students. Who cared what a bunch of judges thought?

On Monday morning, I visited the homerooms of my students to tell them that some important people would be in my classroom that afternoon. I told the students that I knew they would do a great job. I winked at Freddie and smiled to show him that I believed in him. He nodded, knowing that I was speaking directly to him.

By the time three o'clock came, I was ready. My classroom had two doors—one for entering and one for exiting. As I was standing at the entrance greeting the students and the judges, I looked over my shoulder to what should have been empty desks. But to my surprise, Freddie had snuck in through the exit and was the first child in class. His hands were tightly folded on his desk, and his knuckles were white. A frozen smile covered his face, and his eyes and cheeks bulged like a blowfish. Have you ever tried to push a basketball underwater? When you let go, it will fly up into the air. That is the best way to describe Freddie at that moment. It was as if there were an invisible horde of angels there on my behalf, holding him in his seat. If those angels let go, I knew he would just hit the ceiling. But the lesson went beautifully. The students were highly engaged and Freddie was abundantly eager. Throughout the period, I could see the students glancing at him and then at me as if to say, "What is *up* with Freddie?"

At the end of thirty minutes, the judges were to go to a conference room on the other side of the school to complete their evaluations. When we were finished, I asked the class, "Who would like to escort the judges to the conference room?"

Freddie shot his hand up like a missile and waved it back and forth. I scanned the room to look for a more suitable escort, but there was no denying his zeal, and the judges all smiled adoringly at this boy who had been so very charming and perfect throughout the class period. Freddie speedily led them out of the room, causing them to quicken their pace as they left.

To this day, I don't know if he ran with them to that conference room or if he stopped halfway there and pointed them in the right direction, but I do know he came back to my class way too soon. The door shot open and hit the wall, and Freddie burst into the room as only he could do.

"THAT WAS THE LONGEST HOUR OF MY LIFE!" he shouted while holding his head as if his brain would spontaneously combust. It had only been thirty minutes.

We all burst into contagious laughter. Tears streamed down my face, and the whole class couldn't seem to stop giggling. Finally, after composing myself, I looked at Freddie and said, "You were so wonderful today. I couldn't have asked for a more perfect student. Thank you."

His response? "I had to be good today. I just had to. I just love you so much." I was completely undone.

As with every challenging child, Freddie had made me a better teacher. He wanted to be a good student—the one who would sit perfectly, answer perfectly, and behave perfectly. However, it took every fiber of his being to be that child for just thirty minutes on one day. Maybe those angels had really been whispering in Freddie's ear, telling him that I believed in him and saw the goodness in him.

Since that day, I have often found myself alone in my classroom, sitting in the desks of my students and pondering better ways to develop the relationships that are necessary in order to teach them all well. I don't always find it easy to love some students, but it is something that I actively strive to do. I think about those children who challenge me the most, and I meditate on all that is good within them. I think about their gifts, their talents, their hearts, and I remind myself that they, too, are God's children and that He has a purpose for each of them.

I wish that I had truly understood this before I started

teaching. If I had, things might have gone differently with Mitchell.

I taught Mitchell my very first year in the classroom, and when he entered each day, students would quickly scurry off to their desks. I wanted to do the same thing. Mitchell's massive frame towered above me, and his perpetual smirk and disdain for authority caused my heart to race and my palms to sweat as I feebly attempted to convince myself that I was in charge. Mitchell had mastered the art of eye rolling and spreading negativity, and I struggled to remain enthusiastic during lessons when he was present. When he would sigh and slump in his chair, an ominous cloud covered my class, and despite my attempts to keep him in line, I made countless rookie mistakes with him.

"Mitchell, please return to your seat," I'd say.

"I wasn't doing anything! I just needed to throw something away," he'd respond.

"Mitchell, please stop talking while I am talking!" I'd plead.

"I wasn't talking!" he'd reply, despite the fact that I had seen him.

"Mitchell, don't do that," I'd say, as my voice would crack.

"What? I didn't do anything wrong. You are always picking on me!" he'd argue.

You get the picture. He made me want to scream and run out of the room, or at the very least, repeatedly bang my head against the wall. Mitchell always had an excuse, and I was inconsistent when issuing consequences. I'm sure that he also sensed my dislike. If you had asked me about him then, I would have told you that his sole mission on earth was to make every day a living hell for me. As the year progressed, my confidence increased and I learned how to more firmly issue consequences for misbehavior, yet it was always a struggle that left me exhausted. We made it through that year, and at the end, I was relieved to see him go. I thought that I wouldn't have to deal with him again and that he would be out of my life for good.

Eight years later, Mitchell took his own life.

I didn't learn about Mitchell's death until several years after it took place and it still haunts me to this day. I'm sure I was just one of many people in Mitchell's life who had trouble with him, and I can't help but wonder what would have happened if someone had seen him differently. To this day I do not know all the details of what led to his brokenness. When I taught Mitchell, I did not know anything about his home situation. I did not know what he loved, and I did not know what moved him. I never asked him about his hobbies, and I cannot remember if I ever gave him a sincere, meaningful compliment about anything. I never tried to figure out why he was so angry, and I never showed him the love that he was desperate to receive. As a first-year teacher, I focused only on how he made me feel instead of his apparent cries for help. I never once tried to develop a meaningful relationship, and now, twenty-six years later, I can't forgive myself for it.

I failed you, Mitchell, and I am so sorry.

I will not make this mistake again. Relationship building isn't always easy, but I have learned that it is the single most effective way to engage and motivate my students. Though I am clearly the teacher and they are the students, I can still let them know that I care for them and that I'm trying to understand them. This kind of attention has a profound impact on their ability to grow.

Several years after teaching Mitchell, I taught Jeremy, a country boy who had little interest in academics. Quiet and sullen, Jeremy slouched at his desk with his long bangs covering his eyes. When called upon he would answer in his heavy drawl, "I daunt know, ma'am." He took no initiative and all his comments had to be solicited from me. When it came to homework, I was dismayed by his lack of effort, and it pained me to see how low his grades were. I knew that Jeremy was smart. I guess some would simply label him as lazy.

At this point, I had been teaching for a few years and I had a good repertoire of strategies for even the most reluctant learners. In fact, Jeremy happened to be in a class full of students who were highly engaged in my lessons. But I just couldn't figure out how to inspire him. One day when I kept him after class I decided to change my approach.

"Jeremy, what do you love?" I asked.

"Ma'am? What d' ya mean?" he asked.

"What do you love to do? What do you get excited about? I have taught you language arts lessons using football, basketball, food, popular television shows, books, games, music, and more. I have tried to use things that my students love, yet you seem completely unimpressed by them all. I want you to love learning, Jeremy, so I need to know what does get your interest."

He stared at me for a moment, and I just stared back and waited.

"Fishin'," he said. "I love fishin'."

"Okay. Then fishing it is."

That night was a long one for me. Right after school I made a few stops and picked up wooden dowels, string, magnets, and metal washers. After some experimentation I had it all figured out. Late that night I loaded my daughter Madison's baby pool into the car. I arrived early the next morning to reserve the gymnasium and to set it all up.

When Jeremy's class arrived, I was ready.

"Everyone, leave all your things here. We are going to do our lesson in the gym today."

The students scurried with me to the gym and gathered around me as I explained the task.

"Guess what? Today we will be speed fishing!" I revealed.

"Speed fishing? What on earth is that?" Ansley asked.

"Well, you will be placed into relay teams. When it is your turn, you will cast your line into the pool. The magnet on the line will function as a fishhook. In this pool there are over one hundred paper fish, each with a metal washer on the back of it. Each fish also has a different word written on it. After you catch a fish, you must then run with it to the other side of the gym, where you will find several plates for your team. You must put your fish on the appropriate plate, based upon which part of speech it is. Then the next member of your team will cast. You will receive a point for each correctly placed fish. You must move quickly and accurately. Are you ready?"

"Yes!" they all exclaimed.

"This is so cool!" added Andrew.

Once I heard their enthusiasm I told them, "You all need to thank Jeremy. He gave me this great idea!"

They all high-fived and clapped for Jeremy, and he smiled broadly with reddened cheeks.

"When you hear the music, you may begin. On your mark, get set . . . go!" I yelled while cuing a twangy country music song on the sound system. Cheering and laughing, the kids raced with intensity as they completed the game. When I dismissed the class that day, Jeremy lingered behind. As he walked past me, he looked up, brushed his long bangs aside, and with smiling eyes stuttered, "Um . . . thanks for today. That was . . . uh, pretty fun."

After that day, things gradually changed with Jeremy. He seemed to realize that I cared about him and that I truly wanted him to love learning. He laughed more, he smiled more, and he participated more with each passing day. It took a little longer for his schoolwork to improve, but he was receptive to my urging and even started to ask for help.

The game I created lasted only twenty minutes, but it changed Jeremy for the entire year. Speed fishing. Who knew?

When we show others that their interests matter to us, we are making meaningful steps toward developing lasting bonds and trust. At the Ron Clark Academy, we make it our business to show the kids that we love many of the things that they love. Every year, our staff works hard to create a joyful welcome to uplift our students on the initial day of school and to celebrate what lies ahead. We plan something special—some sort of surprise. One year we embraced the students' love for roller skating. We borrowed roller skates, and as the students arrived, the twenty staff members rolled up, hugged them, and led them to our makeshift arena where they, too, were able to skate with one another. One year we filled the parking lot with donated inflatable slides and other carnival games, and another year we held a black-light dance party: the students, dressed in all white, were surprised when our darkened library was filled with neon artwork and a pulsating laser light show. But I will never forget what we did for the fall of 2011.

As our students arrived on the first day that year, they were greeted by a one-hundred-piece marching band and college students from the drum lines and step teams at Morehouse, Spelman, Georgia State, and Clark Atlanta University. Our students love stepping, and our school step team, the Essentials, is extraordinary. If you have not seen this sort of dance, it is an art form predominantly practiced by African-American sororities and fraternities; its roots originate in Africa with the Welly "gumboot" dance. When teams step, it is a powerful mixture of clapping, stomping, dancing, and chanting with military-like precision. Step teams also have a long tradition of community service, and so we thought that it would be wonderful for these college students to serve as role models and to celebrate stepping with our kids. But then an even bigger idea started to form in my head. Okay, I admit it . . . as a young woman at the University of Georgia, I was completely mesmerized by the step teams. I thought that it was the most unique type of performance I'd ever seen, and it was even more intriguing because I had never done it. So when we met to plan during the summer, I asked our faculty and staff, "What if *we* put on a step show for the kids on the first day of school?"

Although some of the staff feared that they might lack the skills, everyone agreed to give it a try. And so it was. In the two weeks leading up to the first day of school, we regularly met for practices. We stomped, we sweated, we chanted, and we moaned. Mostly, we laughed. Admittedly, our bodies were a little old for the activity—I proudly earned a bruise on my right thigh that looked just like Italy. But we were motivated to keep practicing until we mastered our routine because we knew the kids would love it. Whether I was in the shower, or in the line at the post office, I found myself stomping and clapping to get it just right.

When the big day arrived, we were as geared up as Beyoncé at the Super Bowl. As the students waited patiently in the lobby, each of us slid down the slide (an RCA tradition). As we came out, the students saw that we were dressed in special black T-shirts with our step nicknames on the back. We started a cheer and then I yelled, *"Set!"* at the top of my lungs. We snapped to attention, and the crowd went wild.

We danced with our arms and feet in sync, heads snapping to attention, chants shouted in unison, formations completed with precision. The show was seven minutes of adrenaline-filled power. We had the time of our lives. When we finished, the students surrounded us, celebrating with high-fives, hugs, cheers, and smiles.

Afterward, when we talked about the experience as a staff, we realized that we felt a bittersweet sadness, knowing that it was all over. The time working on the performance had been a wonderful bonding activity for us because we had helped each other every step of the way. Despite the hard work, we had benefited more than we had ever intended and we will carry the fond memories with us forever. When we stretch to develop relationships with others, we are often uplifted in the most remarkable ways.

The chemistry I create with my students is the primary element that affects my ability to guide them, mold them, and help them find success. And through these relationships, I have learned how to develop better bonds with my loved ones, peers, and colleagues as well. Meaningful relationships do not just "happen." The most powerful relationships occur when we willingly give of ourselves and seek to understand others wholeheartedly.

CLASS NOTES

- If you believe in someone, they are more apt to believe in themselves.
- When we build relationships with others, we are better able to motivate them to reach their fullest potential.
- Those who are the most difficult to love often need love the most.
- When we find it hard to like others, we must seek to focus on their gifts, talents, and goodness.
- If you want to know what matters to someone else, take the time to ask.
- When we go above and beyond for others, it shows our commitment to developing a meaningful relationship.

HOMEWORK

1. Make a list of the people who are in need of a more meaningful relationship with you. Next to each name, list the barriers to that relationship—the things that annoy or frustrate you the most. Then, make a list of the individual's good qualities. Think of ways to break the barriers, and try to focus on that list of good qualities whenever you are dealing with him or her.

2. Take time to deepen your relationships with your children, spouse, or significant other by learning to love some of the things that they love.

3. Ask your loved ones what things matter to them the most, and use that information to plan a special outing, gift, or moment for them. Don't wait for a birthday or special celebration; make it spontaneous.

2

MAGIC

========= COURSE DESCRIPTION =========
In this course, you will learn how to enchant students and help
them see the wonder that is all around them.

I sighed and shook the water from my umbrella and raincoat
as I entered Mr. Clark's class, ready to pick up the fifth graders
and escort them to my room.

"Mrs. Bearden, what on earth is wrong?" he asked.

"It's raining in my room again!"

"Again?" he asked.

"Yes," I sighed. "Mr. Mills and I have been trying to fix it,
but we just can't get it to stop. We will just have to make the
most of it."

"Kids," Mr. Clark went on, "this is a really old building, and lots of strange things happen here. You need to be aware that sometimes it just rains in these rooms."

Without skipping a beat, the students responded in unison, "Yes, sir!"

As they walked down the hall in single file, I saw them look up at the beams of sunlight flowing through the skylight. They looked to the windows, only to see even more sunshine. Their perplexed expressions tickled me.

Dramatizing my exasperation, I continued in my flustered state until we got to the blackened doors of my classroom. "Before you enter, students, I need you to understand that it is pretty bad in there. I have put rain ponchos on your chairs, and there are some glow sticks to help you see. Girls, cover your hair. I'm sorry if you get soaked before lunch. We will just have to make the best of the situation."

The students nodded. A few of them smirked with skepticism; others were wide-eyed with mouths agape. Louis bit his fingernails. And then, we slowly entered the dark room.

KABOOM! Crrrcckkk! Sounds of thunder booming, lightning striking, and torrential rain falling filled the air.

The kids hit the fog-covered floor.

"Mrs. Bearden, it really is raining! Help us!" Jamal exclaimed.

"We will get struck by lightning in here!" shrieked Brielle.

"Kids, it's okay! You won't get struck—I promise. Let's get to our desks. We need to write about this right away so that others will believe it actually happened!"

I suppressed my laughter, and as they scurried for their ponchos, I couldn't wait for the lesson to begin.

"Mrs. Bearden, this paper is soaked with grammatical errors!" joked Kendall.

Brandon exclaimed, "Help, Mrs. Bearden! All of my ideas have evaporated!"

Lauren added, "Hush! I've got my own drought to deal with over here."

"All right, all right. Pretty good," I said, laughing. "I forecast that you will get an F and my storm will worsen if you don't focus and get to work!"

We live in a world that is full of magic, and we all have the ability to create it. That lesson took some simple sound effects, a fog machine, rain ponchos, and glow sticks from the dollar store. But to my students, it was a magical day when it rained in Mrs. Bearden's room. They were willing to suspend reality and simply believe.

We all need a little magic in our lives—we need to allow ourselves to imagine, to dream, to delight in a world that is full of mystical wonder. When we are young, we revel in fairy tales; we talk to the invisible and even imagine that we hear them answer. I believe that we can still capture the joy that comes from these illusions and experience them as adults. We just have to stop taking ourselves so darn seriously and let go of our adult logic.

What is the best way for an adult to experience magic? At RCA, we try to produce students who take pleasure in the wonder and glory that come with an unbridled imagination. With this in mind, we buried a mystery within the school, waiting to be discovered.

When we were in the midst of transforming a hundred-year-old factory into the Ron Clark Academy, Ron told me his plan to place permanent clues throughout the building with the hope that one day a curious student would unlock them and find the hidden surprise. Each coded clue leads to another. One student has found five clues; no one has gotten any further. Not one child has unlocked all twelve steps to discover where the treasure lies.

So each year, we tell our students the story of the clues and how one must follow them in order to find the hidden mystery. This year, our fifth-grade class was especially intrigued by the whole idea.

"Is it dangerous?"

"How will we know when we find it?"

"When do we go looking for it?"

"Will you *pleeaasse* tell us what it is?"

Ron explained the rules: "You must figure out times to look for clues, but of course you cannot miss class to do so. You cannot share the clues with anyone else, and you might get into trouble if you go looking and are gone for too long. You will find clues where something just doesn't look like it should, so be very observant at all times."

Intrigued, they all leaned in closer, firing off more questions.

"Can we take a friend with us to find it?"

"How do I go looking for it and not get into trouble?"

Joyfreda suddenly sat upright and thrust her arm into the air, obviously struck by an important revelation.

"Yes, Joyfreda?" I asked.

"Mrs. Bearden, are we permitted to carry a flashlight with us at all times, just in case we need to use it?"

"Why, yes, Joyfreda. That is permitted," I responded.

If you ever visit RCA, you might notice some of our students with flashlights sticking out of their pockets, looking for things that just aren't the way that they should be. They study the walls, the halls, the lockers, the ceilings. They peek into passageways and under furniture, hoping to find the next clue. One day, some child will discover the secret. In the meantime, the beauty of the mystery lies in their brilliant imaginations.

When I see my students' faces sparkle with curiosity, I can't help but think of how much of this imaginative energy is lost on us as adults and I am reminded of how school often destroys this sense of wonder. We teach that there is always one right answer, one way to think, and one way to perform, and in doing so we create a society of children who trade in their uniqueness to conform to a certain standard. I have had the opportunity to visit schools all over this country and on six continents—all but Antarctica. And you can identify a school that stifles imagination as soon as you walk through the hallways—the joy is missing. On the other hand, schools that embrace the spirit of magic seem to emit a special energy. Unfortunately, this doesn't just happen with the flourish of a wand. But when we take the time to create the illusion, the results are worth every effort we've made. I have even taken my students on a journey to another planet . . . without ever leaving my classroom.

Cautiously, my students entered the darkened foyer. Unsure of what awaited them, they whispered and huddled together as they tiptoed into the blackness. They knew that I was up to something. After emerging from the dense fog surrounding the doorway, my students found glowing neon planets floating above them, sparkling stars on dark walls, and alien eyes peeking out from every corner. Laser beams filled the air, and glow sticks illuminated their desks. Ethereal music was accompanied by the distant sounds of spaceships. The kids were disoriented and in total awe.

Dressed in full alien garb, I could only speak to them through my "interplanetary translation apparatus," a device that distorted my voice so that it sounded more like an alien's. The students jumped when they first saw me and quickly felt their way to their seats. As I introduced myself as Princess Orion from the planet Ooloo, they hung on every word. I spun a tale about how their spacecraft had been shot down during the great Interplanetary War, and that they might be stuck here awhile.

Suddenly a large interactive whiteboard screen in the front of the room came to life. I had covered the edges of it with foil to convince the students that it was a part of the ship that had made it through the terrible crash, and it would enable Star Fleet (my students) to communicate with Commander Bearden at NASA's mission intelligence station. You see, I had taped videos of myself ahead of time, and I pretended to be in a control room, frantic with worry. I set these videos to pop up throughout the lesson as if I were communicating with the students, live from NASA.

"Star Fleet, this is Commander Bearden at mission control. We cannot locate your craft. Repeat. We cannot locate your craft! Our intergalactic geographic tracking device has malfunctioned and we are unable to plot your location. We lost you sometime after you entered the Tritonian Galaxy. Warning, Star Fleet: proceed with caution. The Tritonian Galaxy is known for its very dangerous creatures. Many are rumored to be violent, and they will suck your brains out."

The students cracked up as they held on to their heads to prevent their brains from being devoured. Then Commander Bearden (via video) gave them a series of writing tasks that would be necessary to get home safely. Trouble ensued when the aliens began to intercept my transmissions, and the students had to work even harder to find their way home.

Suddenly, Commander Lokey (my fellow teacher Rhonda) burst into the room, frantic with relief at finding the surviving members of Star Fleet. As she dramatically asked for their account of what had transpired, the students shared their dilemma with her. They then all turned to me, Princess Orion, and began to interrogate me.

Using my interplanetary translation apparatus, I explained that I meant them no harm. However, it was likely that they had been shot down in the Interplanetary War. Our planet had formed an alliance with planets in opposition to the powers trying to overtake us. As I spun a wonderful tale about the casualties of the battle, Elijah exclaimed, "Wait! That same thing happened on *our* planet!"

Rhonda had actually been teaching about World War I in her class, and we both swallowed a laugh at Elijah's epiphany. He got it. All of the kids did, and they played right along with great intensity. I have not found more fascinating compare-and-contrast essays than the ones that our students wrote about World War I and the Interplanetary War. That day, our imaginations transported us to another galaxy, one where anything was possible.

This collective commitment to creating magic permeates our school, and it begins with our staff. We support each other in our quest to make each classroom come alive. Together, we realize the power of instilling such joyful experiences in the hearts of our students; the magic ignites a fire for learning deep within them. Can you imagine getting excited about learning the rules for using gerunds? Well, my students did when I transformed my classroom into the House of Ing.

Chinese lanterns illuminated the room full of red dragons, fans, and white tablecloths topped with red takeout boxes and platters. I cued my music and double-checked each red box to make sure that it contained sentence strips with gerunds, words that look like verbs but function as nouns. (Gerunds usually end in -*ing,* hence the name the House of Ing!)

Each student would learn how to use chopsticks to remove the sentence strips and place them onto the correct platter— gerunds as subjects, gerunds as predicate nominatives, gerunds as direct objects, or gerunds as objects of prepositions. They would then sequence the strips in each platter to learn more about China. The room looked perfect—I thought that the kids would love it. As I opened my bag of chopsticks to complete my setup, I realized that there was a problem.

Mr. Bernadin saw me frowning as he entered the room to let me know that it was time to greet the teachers who would be observing our classrooms that day.

"Mrs. Bearden, what is wrong? You look frustrated!" he said.

"Well, yes, I am. I wanted to make this lesson magical for the kids, and well, somehow using pencils as chopsticks takes away from it all. I needed thirty sets of chopsticks, not thirty total—I guess that I didn't communicate very effectively!" I sighed. "It's okay—I will make do."

Ron and I went to greet the visiting educators and review the day's schedule with them. Thirty minutes later, my students and the educators entered the House of Ing. As I escorted everyone to their tables, Mr. Bernadin came running into my room and handed me two bags of chopsticks.

"Mr. Bernadin, how did you—"

He just smiled and left before I could finish my question. Afterward I found him to thank him and ask him how he had produced those chopsticks at eight thirty in the morning. Our school is not located anywhere near a Chinese restaurant.

"Well," he said, "when I saw how much you wanted those chopsticks to make it special for the kids, I knew that I just had to make it happen. I jumped in my car and went to three convenience stores. One had a few, but I needed more. At the third store, they had a counter where they actually serve Chinese food sometimes, so I was able to get the rest."

Mr. Bernadin is the technology specialist at our school and we often call him Superman because of his ability to fix any computer problem. On that day, he went above and beyond to create a special moment for our students, without even being asked.

That same year, as part of our commitment to continuous school improvement, we spent several months engaging our staff, parents, board, and other stakeholders in revisiting our school's mission and purpose. The most rewarding part of the exercise came when we asked our eighth-grade students to brainstorm the qualities that they hope all RCA students will carry with them long after they graduate from our school. In small groups the students filled chart paper that we posted around the room, and then we asked them to put stars beside the answers that most strongly resonated with them. As I walked around to see their completed work, I was very pleased and proud of their popular responses, such as *lift up others, have a strong work ethic, study often,* and *give back to the community*. But then I noticed one response that had rows of shimmering gold stars next to it. As I approached, my heart leapt as I saw what was written there: *Believe in the magic that is all around you*.

When we see the world through the eyes of children, we increase our ability to dream and imagine. We don't just see people and situations as they are; we envision all that they can be.

MAGIC

CLASS NOTES

- We live in a world full of magic and wonder. We just need to take the time to embrace it.
- As adults, we often forget the joy that comes with imagining and suspending belief.
- Creating magic for others is worth the effort that it takes.
- When we consider experiences through the perspectives of others, we see potential we would have otherwise missed.

HOMEWORK

1. Reflect on when you were a child. Think about the ways in which you utilized your imagination. Do you still have the ability to use it in the same way?
2. Find ways to engage in imaginative thinking through art, music, or any medium that enables you to delve into your inner child. Take a course if necessary to help you reconnect with that part of you.
3. Brainstorm ways to create magic in the lives of others. Make a point of making moments happen for those you love, especially kids.
4. Make a habit of trying to visualize scenarios through the eyes of others. What do you see that you might have missed before? Use this information to broaden your imagination.

3

COURAGE

===== COURSE DESCRIPTION =====

In this course, you will learn how to face fears
and abandon needless worries.

I was surprised to learn that one of my most athletic students, Aujahuna, had never learned to swim. In fact, she was terrified of the water and was nervous to even try. So when we learned that her class would have an opportunity to go to Australia, we knew that we had to get her lessons. So Ron and I took a group of our students to his parents' home for the weekend. With instruction, patience, and encouragement, Aujahuna eased into the water and learned to make her way around the deep end by holding on to the sides.

Due to the generosity of Delta Air Lines and several other

sponsors, our students had the opportunity to stay in Australian homes and visit Sydney, a rain forest, a remote cattle station, and even the Great Barrier Reef. On a beautiful April morning, my students, teachers, and I boarded a sailboat to go snorkeling in the reef. We laughed, we sang, we cheered, and we hoisted sails as the sun beat down upon us and the wind whipped through our hair. We even tried our darnedest to try to speak with an Australian accent like our guide, Mark (or as he said it, "Maahk").

Our trip to the reef was breathtaking, but we did need to be careful. We had to wear suits that we were told would protect us from jellyfish stings. But despite our fears, we all put on our gear and followed our guides into the magnificent, sparkling ocean. The children's shrieks of joy filled the air:

"Look, I found Nemo!"

"You have to come see this—it looks like moving fingers!"

"Oh my gosh—it's an octopus!"

"Is that a *shark*?" (It actually was, but it left us alone!)

As I looked at the boat, I saw Aujahuna slowly making her descent into the water with the help of one of the guides. She was clearly terrified. She was making quite a leap: going from one night in an eight-foot-deep swimming pool to snorkeling in the Great Barrier Reef was sort of like playing one game of pee-wee football and then starting in the Super Bowl. Of course, there were flotation rings stationed at numerous locations in the water all around the boat to ensure the safety of our students. But as I watched the resolve on Aujahuna's face, I just knew that she was determined to fight her fears and not let this experience pass her by. She put on her mask, lowered her face into the water, and lifted her head back out again to flash a magnificent smile.

How many times have you been too afraid to take part in a life-changing event? Obviously, you don't have to be in Australia to have such a moment. Sometimes it could be as simple as missing an opportunity to try something new, to say how we feel, or to allow ourselves to develop certain relationships. But when we are able to embrace the support of others, take a deep breath, and face our anxieties, the feeling of accomplishment is profound. Sometimes we have to ease in just one step at a time, but as we overcome each small challenge, our courage grows. It is my hope that all of my students will live without fear, no matter how scary the situation.

Haunted, dark, and dangerous, the thought of the RCA boiler room sends shivers up the spines of many of our students, even though no one has ever seen it. Because we are located in a factory building, our school has many hidden nooks, crannies, and passageways, but the boiler room remains a place of school legend. So much so that the students do not go looking for it; in fact, the students have asked me to promise that our school's mystery isn't located in the depths of such evil. Some might say that the room doesn't even exist—that it is a myth perpetuated by the teachers, but what kind of teachers would we be if we did that?

While my staff and I are tickled that thoughts of the boiler room could scare the kids, we try to do all that we can to teach that there is no room for fear in life. And as a result, our students live boldly and embrace all of life's opportunities. In fact, they are the ones who often teach me to abandon worries.

During the fourth week of school, my students gave poetry presentations. They had one week to memorize two poems: one original piece and one written by someone else. There would be no notes, no podium—only a spotlight and a microphone. At RCA we require our students to step out and step up—they must learn to speak not only about academic content, but also about their feelings, beliefs, and insights. They are taught to show the world how incredible they are, even if it pushes them outside their comfort zone. It is okay to be introverted, but every child must be able to communicate effectively.

These poetry presentations were the fifth-grade students' first formal speaking opportunity, and they were very jittery. So, of course, I had to pull from my special bag of tricks to make the day something to be remembered.

"Welcome to Café Latte! My name is Rain," I said, greeting the students while passing out berets and banging on my bongo drum. The students entered my room to find a candlelit café, chocolate milk, and cookies. As sixties jazz music set the tone, the mics were checked, the spotlight set, and the lineup posted. Each student performed two poems—some were artfully delivered; others were a little less impressive. But through it all, my students supported each other and snapped in appreciation for the effort that each poet put forth.

One year later, I was chatting with some of these students about their experiences in the fifth grade. Kamryn said, "Mrs. Bearden, I will never forget our poetry coffeehouse."

"I'm so glad. Why? Did you think it was fun?" I asked.

"Well, it was fun, but I won't forget it because it was the day I faced my fears."

"Really? Why do you say that?"

"Mrs. Bearden, I was terrified to speak in front of people, but you gave me no choice. I practiced at home in my bedroom every night so that I wouldn't completely freeze and forget my lines. When I recited my poem for the class, it wasn't perfect, but I was *sooo* proud of myself because I did it. It was one of my proudest moments. Now I really enjoy speaking in front of other people."

As I absorbed her comments, Michael added, "Yes, Mrs. Bearden. That day helped me overcome a fear, too."

Michael is a huge extrovert, so I thought that he was kidding. "Michael, now I know that you weren't afraid of talking in front of people. I had to work to get you to *stop* talking on the very first day of school!" I laughed.

"Oh, no, ma'am! I wasn't afraid to speak. I do like to hear myself! But I had always loved to write poetry. I was afraid that others would think that it wasn't cool. But I shared my poem that day, and now I am not afraid to tell others that I am a poet. I am proud to be one."

We all have fears—some that we share, and some that we harbor deep inside. As Kamryn and Michael will tell you, it feels good to face our fears; in fact, it even empowers us. And if we can help others overcome their fears, the payoff is even greater.

During that same trip to Australia, some of Aujahuna's classmates needed help fighting fears created by their imaginations when we visited the Woodleigh Cattle Station, a remote ranch in the outback.

"Look out! Please, Mrs. Bearden, can't we walk this way instead?" Dasia implored as we ventured down the dirt path.

"Why does it matter, sweetie?" I said.

"Because you keep going under the trees, and those drop bears will get us!"

"Drop bears? What are you talking about?" I asked. We had studied the animal life in Australia before our trip, but I had no clue what she meant.

Jai helped her explain. "Mrs. Bearden, the owners of the cattle station said that we need to watch out whenever we walk under the trees, or the Australian drop bears will fall on us and attack us. They warned us when we took our tour last night."

"Drop bears?" I questioned.

"Oh, yes, ma'am," Jai went on. "They are vicious and they like to land on people, especially tourists!"

Sure enough, as I looked around, I saw all of the kids scrambling to avoid the trees. We were strolling through a wooded area, and we wanted the opportunity to soak it all in: the cerulean sky, the tall grass, the fresh air. But my students were becoming increasingly more focused on the treetops than on the beauty around us. I watched as they continued to duck and swerve while looking obsessively at the branches overhead. My kids were obviously terrified that they would be the next victims of these horrid creatures. It was hilarious.

I walked to the bottom of a tree, stood under it, and smiled.

"Nooo, don't, Mrs. Bearden! Move! They will get you!" the students exclaimed in unison. Jai, always the protector, ran and tried to pull me into the road.

I burst into laughter. "Guys, there are no drop bears. There is no such thing."

"But the guides said that there were!" Dasia exclaimed.

"Aw, man," responded Jai. "I should have known they were just messing with us. I knew it sounded a little far-fetched. I guess the whole thing does sound a little bit illogical!"

As silly as those drop bears might seem, so are some of our adult fears. It is time to open the boiler room door and peer inside. Stand under a tree and soak it in. Stop allowing your fears to paralyze you from enjoying the magnificent blessings all around you.

CLASS NOTES

- Many of our greatest fears are based on things that aren't even real or that most likely will not happen.
- We must be willing to recognize our deepest fears and face them head-on.
- If we fail to confront our worries and anxieties, we miss out on many of life's most magical moments.
- Teach others to overcome their fears so that they can experience all that life has to offer.

HOMEWORK

1. Make a list of your greatest, deepest fears, and next to each, write the worst thing that could happen if they actually came true. By understanding them, it will allow you to come to peace with them.
2. Reflect upon a time when your fears came true. What did you learn from the experience? How did it make you stronger or wiser?
3. Find ways to help others overcome whatever is holding them back. Support them as they work through the things that paralyze them and keep them from experiencing an abundant life.

4

PLAY

=== COURSE DESCRIPTION ===

In this course, you will learn the benefits of childlike merriment.

Mischievous, joyful, rambunctious, silly—these words describe the eighth-grade boys at a former school where I served as the principal during the eighteenth year of my career. One day, after a week of especially heavy rain, the PE teacher was relieved to have an opportunity to take the class outside for a game of kickball. Walking down the hallway, I was accosted by an exasperated student. "Can you come to the fields right away? Coach Bacon said he needs you right now!"

Off I ran toward the fields, thinking that someone had been injured. But when I arrived, four mud-covered eighth-grade boys greeted me. Coach Bacon was visibly upset, and judging by the boys' slight trembling, they were definitely rattled by his anger.

I used my best principal voice and sternly reprimanded them. "How on earth did this happen? What were you doing? What were you thinking? You are covered—I can't even let you into the building!"

The boys stood nodding their heads, looking shameful, and giving me the obligatory "Yes, ma'am's," and "We're sorry's." As the mud started to harden on their panic-stricken faces, it became increasingly more difficult for them to speak. They looked so absurd that I had to swallow my laughter.

As the story went, it all started when the boys had looked at each other, to the huge mud pit, and back at each other in agreement. Before they knew it, they all had dived in and rolled around while having a grand time.

I looked at Billy and said, "Didn't you realize that you'd get in huge trouble for this?"

"Um, yes, ma'am, we did. But it was just such a big pile of mud, and it was so tempting that I think we all just decided that jumping in it would be so much fun that it would be worth the consequences." At least he was honest. How could I not love that kid?

I took the boys to the side of the school and attempted to hose them off before bringing them inside. After using a ream of paper towels, I took them to the nurse's office to put on the school uniforms that she kept on hand for emergencies. There was only one problem: these boys were now thirteen to fourteen years old, ready to graduate from middle school, and we didn't have anything that was large enough. The only options available fit them like capris and baby doll T-shirts. They had to walk like Frankenstein so that their pants wouldn't tear.

They looked ridiculous, and I couldn't hold it in any longer. I burst out laughing and was followed by the school nurse, the bookkeeper, the coach, and everyone else who saw them. By this point, the boys realized that it would be okay to laugh, too. Making those eighth-grade boys wear those uniforms the rest of the day would be punishment enough. They were mortified, but they were grateful that I didn't suspend them so they took it all in stride.

Now the message here is not that it is okay to teach kids that if something is tempting, you do it despite the circumstances—I am big on teaching kids the consequences of their actions. But sometimes those simple little pleasures can be worth the risk. Those middle school boys knew that rolling in that mud would be an absolute blast. I'll admit that even a part of me wanted to jump into that pit, too. The students were disciplined and they did have consequences, but it was okay that we laughed at the absurdity of it all. And at least Billy told the truth and didn't try to lie his way out of it. These boys have all grown into fine young men. However, I bet that they never forgot the day they took that dive.

As adults, we become so caught up in the stress of our everyday responsibilities that we forget how to just relax; we fail to embrace the idea of playfulness. I am not referring to adult partying here. I am talking about the purity of silliness and interaction just for the sake of having joyful experiences with one another. My students have taught me that when I allow myself to let go, I am able to engage with them on yet another level. When was the last time that you doubled over with gut-wrenching laughter? When was the last time that your cheeks hurt from smiling? Remember how that feels? There is room for silliness in all of our lives. We just have to make it happen.

One afternoon when I escorted my fifth-grade class to Mr. Clark's room, I discovered that he was running late from a meeting.

"Have a seat, kids," I said, "and I will teach you math until Mr. Clark arrives."

"You will teach us *math?*" Symphoni inquired.

"Yes, darling, language arts teachers do know how to do math. I tell you what—I can even do it just like Mr. Clark!" I jumped on the desk and launched into an algebraic problem, à la Ron Clark.

"Class, where do we begin?" I asked.

"Parentheses!" they all exclaimed together.

"Because?"

"When we begin, we begin together; parentheses first now please be clever!" we all sang in unison.

I did my darnedest to impersonate Mr. Clark as the students giggled and we worked the problem. Three minutes in, I saw Mr. Clark standing in the doorway with an arched eyebrow and a bemused grin.

"Um, hello, Mr. Clark! Time to go!" I said, feigning panic and running for the door. The students all covered their mouths to suppress their laughter.

"Oh no you don't!" he said. "Two can play this game. Have a seat!"

Mr. Clark tossed his imaginary long hair back and forth, walked like me in high heels, and impersonated me teaching a grammar lesson. I had to admit it was pretty hilarious, but I pretended to be offended and went after him with a yardstick.

He grabbed a yardstick, too, and we began to duel. "En garde!" he said as we battled. The children shouted and cheered with delight. We chased each other around the room, over and under desks, as the students darted out of the way, shrieking dramatically.

Finally, Mr. Clark knocked my ruler sword out of my hand. Completely winded, I reached out, grabbed his yardstick, and broke it in half over my knee as the children cheered and we both took a bow. The whole exchange lasted two minutes, but it was an unforgettable incident.

Several months later, the students in that same class were given a writing assignment: "What Makes a Great Teacher?" I was curious to see what our students would say after spending their first year at RCA, and I thought their input would help me continue to grow as an educator.

The beautifully written essays included many insightful points about caring, smiling, encouraging, pushing, helping, and even disciplining children. But it was Jacobi's paper that spoke to me the loudest. He asked if he could read it to the class, and I obliged.

Jacobi is a very precocious, funny young man who would make a great game show host. With his own flair for the dramatic, he approached the stage, emphatically cleared his throat, and began.

"Hmmm . . . ," he said, putting his finger to his chin and

looking up into the air in thought, "what makes a great teacher, you ask? Well, a great teacher enforces rules, but breaks rulers."

That was all I heard as he continued to read. I swallowed back tears as the class applauded for Jacobi's essay and then began to share their memories of the infamous swordfight.

Jacobi reminds us that children need both structure and play. Sometimes it is the spontaneous, silly moments that really matter to children. I would argue that my students and I are even better equipped to learn together because we know how to play together. The bond that we form when we play enables the joy to translate to education.

A few weeks after that swordfight, those students reclined on their towels and inhaled the fresh salt air. Crashing waves thundered in the distance, and calypso drum music surrounded us. Brandon put his ear to a massive conch shell while Angelina and Alonzo ran their fingers through the sand in their buckets.

"Please pass the sunscreen," Lauren said to Hannah.

"I need some, too, please!" added Nichcolas. "I can smell it a whole lot better if I put it on my nose!"

Michael joked, "Mrs. Bearden, I hope that we don't get burned!"

Brendon added, "It's a good thing we have these sunglasses. It is really bright!"

"Yes, Mrs. Bearden," added Shawl. "The light—um, the sunlight—is intense."

While we relaxed on our own private beach inside my classroom, I taught the students about onomatopoeia, alliteration, personification, similes, metaphors, and imagery. The walls faded away as we imagined the ocean reaching as far as the eye could see. We didn't notice the ceiling, the floor, the windows, or the doors . . . We were swept away by our imagination.

Kyndall said, "Mrs. Bearden, the waves are reaching their fingertips across the golden sand!"

"The ocean is like a war as each wave battles and retreats in an attempt to gain precious land," shared Louis.

"Yea, and it's causing me to get sand in my swimsuit!" joked Brandon.

And so the students continued to use figurative language to write magnificent poetry about their day at the ocean. At the end of the class, Brielle said, "Thank you, Mrs. Bearden, for letting us play on the beach all period!"

Nichcolas added, "Wait—I just realized something. We learned a whole lot today! You made us think that we were just playing, but we were really learning all along. Sneaky!"

I smiled and nodded as they all laughed. Yes, we played. And yes, we learned a whole lot at the same time. What could be better?

In my younger years, I took myself far too seriously. But once the children in my life taught me how to play, I learned how to lighten up, loosen up, and live more. It is my hope that you will take time to do the same.

CRASH COURSE

───────────── CLASS NOTES ─────────────

- Sometimes in life, we have to learn to dive in and take a chance, just for the fun of it.
- It is important to find the humor in life's silly adventures.
- Adults need to embrace silliness, just for the sake of sharing in their students' joyful experiences.
- When we take time to play with children, we show them how to enjoy simple pleasures.
- Play can be a meaningful way to learn.

───────────── HOMEWORK ─────────────

1. Think back to your childhood and reflect upon instances when you enjoyed playing with others. When was the last time you allowed yourself to play in that way? How can you incorporate this fun into your everyday adult life?
2. The next time your child asks you to play a game or throw a ball, don't tell them you are too busy. Put aside the work and take time for the interaction.
3. Find creative ways to combine play with learning, such as teaching integers while playing football together or by reviewing spelling words while playing freeze tag.
4. Stop taking yourself too seriously. Really.

5

RECOVERY

========= COURSE DESCRIPTION =========
In this course, you will learn how to absorb blows and recover from
bad breaks or mistakes.

The first time I encountered Mr. Fields, I wilted like a flower.
Mr. Fields was the father of Jesse Fields, a fidgety, rude student
whom I taught twenty-seven years ago during my very first year
in the classroom. Jesse was a little kid who carried himself with
a bravado that often left his classmates cowering with fear. His
words could sting, and he had the ability to totally disarm both
students and adults alike with his biting insults.

Jesse's comments were a constant challenge to all the teachers. I had been teaching school for a total of six weeks when
Jesse called a student an inappropriate name while exiting the

classroom. I issued Jesse a detention for after school on the following day. Though visibly unhappy about this punishment, he promptly appeared at dismissal the next afternoon.

Forty-five minutes into the assigned one-hour detention, a large, angry father stood at my door. He wore a flannel T-shirt, jeans, work boots, and a baseball cap emblazoned with the rebel flag.

"Where's the teacher?" he boomed.

Gulp.

"Oh, hello, Mr. Fields. I am Jesse's teacher. It is so nice to meet you." I held out my hand, but he didn't return the gesture.

"*You* are the teacher? You look like one of them students. What's your problem with my boy?"

"Well, Mr. Fields, Jesse used unacceptable language, and so our school policy requires that he be issued a detention."

"Well, sounds like you are picking on my boy to me. Why's he failing your class? My boy is going to get a football scholarship, and I'm not about to let you ruin it for him!" He was now yelling, and as he berated me, Jesse just sat there with a satisfied, smug grin on his face.

I was reduced to Jell-O.

My twenty-one-year-old self quivered and blinked back tears. My voice cracked as I meekly attempted to explain the situation: "Mr. Fields, your son hasn't turned in several assignments."

"My boy did the work. Now are you calling him a liar?"

"Um, no, sir, but in addition to doing the work, he actually has to turn in the work. We are trying to teach him to be responsible and independent."

This exchange went back and forth until Mr. Fields finally

left in disgust. As soon as he and Jesse exited the building, I ran to the principal's office and broke down into sobs. Yes, I did the ugly cry. As I was trying to relay the horror of it all through my hysterical rant, we looked up to see Mr. Fields standing in the doorway again. (He really did move quietly for such a large man. Maybe he was a Navy SEAL before.)

His demeanor was vastly different now as he said, "Why don't I just lean over now so you two can kick me in the butt?"

My principal replied, "Excuse me?"

"Look, you didn't have to go and call the police on me. I just get a little worked up over my boy, that's all. I'm sorry for yellin'."

Perhaps it was divine intervention; or maybe it was merely luck, but a police car had pulled up in front of the school just as Mr. Fields was leaving. It scared him right out of his rebel hat, which he now took off as he bowed to issue an apology.

My principal firmly thanked Mr. Fields for his apology and stated that he would not tolerate him speaking to his teachers in a disrespectful manner. He also reiterated that he supported my decisions regarding his son, and that if he had any other areas of concern, then he should set up an appointment.

"Yes, sir!" Mr. Fields said while he promptly scurried out the door.

After he left, I couldn't help but laugh through my tears. As I finally pulled myself together, my principal kindly comforted me, but he also explained how I should have never, ever allowed myself to be treated that way. As soon as Mr. Fields entered and spoke rudely to me, I should have asked him to schedule a conference, wait outside, or go to the front office. Standing there and allowing him to yell at me in front of his son was just about the worst thing I could have done, for I had allowed Mr. Fields to undermine my authority as the teacher. My lack of confidence in myself had allowed me to go against my instincts, even though I knew that my decisions regarding Jesse had been right. I ended up learning a lot that year as a teacher, and I even connected with Jesse after the first few road bumps.

It is also funny how sometimes our path leads us to cross others more than once. Over the course of the years that passed, I had often thought about that incident and was still embarrassed by it. A full ten years later, I was working at another middle school at the opposite end of our district. The now thirty-one-year-old version of me was boxing up books for the summer when I heard a vaguely familiar voice.

"Uh . . . didn't you used to teach my son?"

I looked up to see Mr. Fields standing there again, but this time, he didn't seem nearly as large. In fact, he seemed quite ordinary, with his shoulders slumped, and the anger in his voice had been replaced by sadness, or so it seemed.

"Mr. Fields? Uh . . . my goodness. How are you?"

"I'm fine, ma'am. I'm just here to do some summer maintenance on the building."

"How is Jesse?"

"Well, he is good I reckon. He has a good job working in an auto shop. Guess that football scholarship wasn't meant to be. Me and his mom divorced a few years ago—he lives with her."

"Well, Mr. Fields, please tell him that I said hello when you talk to him."

"Yes, ma'am." He turned to leave, but he stopped short in the doorway and added, "I know that I talked real ugly to you before, and I want to apologize."

"No worries, Mr. Fields. It's ancient history." We smiled at one another, and as he walked away, tears pooled in my eyes. I now felt nothing but compassion for this troubled man—a man who now seemed so broken and small. I now know that he really just wanted a good life for his son, despite his inappropriate actions.

I also realized that I had allowed that incident to haunt me for far too long. I had fostered a mixture of resentment, embarrassment, and insecurity over the whole thing instead of just learning from it and letting it go. Too often we harbor anger toward others, and it eats away at our core. Now I know how to have a compassionate and understanding spirit when dealing with difficult people in any situation. It feels awful to be blasted by someone in an email or to have someone speak rudely to you, and it isn't acceptable. But responding with anger or not letting go of the situation doesn't improve the outcome. We must forgive and learn from the encounter. And at times, we need to reassure the other individual that the whole thing is in the past.

Case in point: Last winter, my sixth-grade class was blessed to be sponsored for a trip to Park City, Utah, by one of our school's dear friends and supporters, Jeff Anderson. For the past six years, Mr. Anderson has graciously invited our students to his home where we spend the weekend learning to ski, tube, sled, and make snowballs. (There is definitely an art to snowball making that most children from Georgia don't know.) The trip is always filled with laughter and great fun as the students struggle to excel at these new winter sports.

On the first morning there, we rose early, eager to see the freshly fallen powder and head over to the ski resort for the day. As we anxiously layered our snow gear and prepared to depart, I continued to fight the feeling that something was wrong—horribly wrong—with me. I felt dizzy, feverish, and queasy. Before long, I couldn't deny it any longer: I was sick. Terribly sick. I will spare you the details.

So as my precious children headed to the slopes with Ron and the other chaperones, I was forced to stay in bed all day, holding both a bucket and my own private pity party. Over the next two days, I remained bedridden, missing out on all the fun. Mr. Anderson offered to take me to the hospital, but the long drive down winding mountain roads sounded torturous, so I opted to tough it out.

I asked one request of the students: Please, please, let me sleep it off. Stay very quiet. Have you ever stayed in a cabin with thirty twelve-year-olds? It was stupid of me to expect them to be quiet. But with every door slammed, I grew more and more upset. Each loud explosion of laughter created fury in me. And to make matters worse, by the time we had to head back to Atlanta, I discovered I was too sick to travel with the kids and was forced to remain there an additional day.

At our school we are big on teaching our students to respect others' homes and to always pick up after themselves. So when

I saw the mess the students left behind in their excitement, I was dumbfounded. I took pictures of their offenses: wet towels left on beds, trash beside the trash can, and more. When I returned to school, I showed the pictures to the students and openly expressed my disappointment.

The students apologized profusely, which made me quickly forget about the whole thing. It was time for Christmas break, after all! Incidentally, after we returned from vacation, my schedule changed and the sixth grade started classes with our other language arts teacher, Mrs. Barnes, so that I could add the eighth grade to my schedule.

Two months passed, and as always, whenever I saw the sixth-grade students in the hall, I smiled and hugged them. However, I was struck by the fact that they often seemed a little down and less energetic than the class I knew and loved. One day Mr. Clark was having a meeting with that same group and asked them how things were going. He was shocked when more than one kid said, "We wish Mrs. Bearden wasn't still mad at us about Utah. We feel really bad about it."

"Mrs. Bearden isn't still mad at you! Why would you think such a thing?" he asked.

"Well, she doesn't want to teach us anymore," they replied.

The two events had nothing to do with each other, yet my students had held that feeling for two full months. It broke my heart when Ron told me, so the next day I headed into his class to set the record straight.

"Hey, y'all," I started, while smiling. "Mr. Clark shared with me that some of you all are still worried that I am thinking about what happened in Utah and that I am still mad about it." Several students nodded at me through teary eyes. "Guys, I haven't ever thought about it again. How many of you have made your parents mad?" They all raised their hands. "Well, your lack of consideration made me mad, and I was delirious and emotional. Don't your parents get over it and move on the next day?" They nodded again. "Honestly, I can barely remember the whole thing! I might not like something that you do, but that doesn't mean that I still don't love you. I am sorry if I made you feel like I didn't care for you anymore. Besides, when I think of you, I think of all of the magical moments we shared over our year and a half together. Our relationship is not defined by a forty-eight-hour period when I was running a high fever!"

They all giggled, and their relief was evident.

"So, are you going to ever teach us again?" Daylin asked.

"Of course! Don't you remember that I told you earlier in the fall that I would teach the eighth for a while, but that we would have classes again later on?"

"Oh, yeah!" Suddenly they remembered. They learned, they let go, and the whole thing became ancient history.

If I were to repeat this event again, I still would have pointed out the mistakes the students made when leaving a mess, but I would have made it clear that it was all water under the bridge after we discussed it. Students need to understand that in life we fall, but we must get up, brush ourselves off, and move on.

If you are struggling with feelings of anger, inadequacy, or sadness, it might be because you are really holding on to the past. Look, you might have been seriously wronged; however, holding on to the pain or bitterness will only destroy you.

When my daughter Madison was in kindergarten, she often came home upset because she claimed that her classmate Courtney was mean to her. According to Madison, Courtney bossed her around, told her what to do, and rolled her eyes at her. I was concerned—I certainly didn't want my daughter to be the victim of a bully. I didn't know if I should contact the school about it or not since I wanted Madison to learn how to stand up for herself, and so I guided her on things to say and how to respond to Courtney should the behaviors continue. Madison told me that Courtney made her "miserable." Imagine my surprise when a few weeks later, I received a voice mail from Courtney's mom asking if Madison could come over to play.

When I told Madison, she squealed, "Can I go? It will be so much fun!"

"Huh? You want to go?" I was confused.

"We are now best friends. I can go, can't I?"

Well, Courtney did become one of her best friends all through elementary school—they finally drifted apart when they went to different middle schools. I was taken aback by how quickly Madison was able to put the past behind her and love Courtney—I even had to wonder if she had imagined that Courtney had mistreated her in the first place. Last summer, the two girls reconnected at twenty-two years of age. As they sat in my living room giggling about memories, they brought up kindergarten. I told Courtney that Madison had once claimed that she had been mean, and Courtney laughed, "Oh, Miss Kim, I was horrid to her! I was really, really mean to her until I decided that I wanted to be her friend!" We laughed and laughed. (And for the record, Courtney is now a sweetheart.)

Somehow, kids seem to be far better equipped to let go of bitterness and not hold a grudge. They are quick to forgive, forget, and move on. We should follow their lead. What is done is done. Learn from it and then leave it in the past.

CLASS NOTES

- We must choose not to harbor bitterness or resentment.
- When others treat us badly, it is often out of misdirected anger.
- It is important to learn from our mistakes, let them go, and move on.
- When you forgive someone, assure them that the past is ancient history.
- Children are often better able to release the past; learn from them.

HOMEWORK

1. Make a list of those things that you are unable to let go of, and decide to put them in the past. Write down a lesson learned from each experience. If necessary, do something symbolic, such as: write the things that hinder you on paper and burn them or write them on rocks that you throw into a lake.

2. Ask for forgiveness if you have wronged another. Even if it was a long time ago, seeking forgiveness can release you from the past. If it is someone whom you shouldn't contact (such as an ex who is now married), then write a note that you do not send. Let it be symbolic.

3. Grant forgiveness to others in your life, even those who don't ask for it. Release the emotional holds that you allow them to have on your life.

6

TALENT

========= COURSE DESCRIPTION: =========
In this course, you will learn how to embrace your unique gifts.

Quiet and reserved, Tyreece was one of the more introverted students in my language arts class. His soft-spoken, gentle demeanor set him apart from the more rambunctious boys in the fifth grade, and despite my urging, he was reluctant to voluntarily answer questions. Always polite and compliant, Tyreece was a pleasant child to teach, but it was evident that he wasn't pushing himself academically. As with many introverted children, it takes time and the building of trust to get beneath the surface and connect, and I was working hard to figure out what things made Tyreece tick.

By November, Tyreece was participating more in class,

and he seemed to love the way I integrated music into my lessons. However, the moments of rapt attention were equally balanced by others where Tyreece seemed far, far away. Even his peers were going above and beyond to try to connect with him to no avail; Tyreece was often described as "quirky" or "withdrawn."

So, I was completely startled one December morning when Raven burst into my classroom to find me grading papers. "Mrs. Bearden, Mr. Clark says to come quick! It's Tyreece!"

I leapt up and darted down to Mr. Clark's class. As I burst through the door, I stopped dead in my tracks to find Tyreece standing in front of the room singing, like no child I had ever heard before. The students and Ron's mouths were agape as Tyreece belted out "O Holy Night." Everyone was completely spellbound. He hit each note with perfect clarity and pitch, and when he got to the famous high note at "Oh, night, divine . . ." tears spilled down some of our faces. Definitely mine.

It was so beautiful that when he stopped, it took a good five seconds for us to be transported back to the classroom and start clapping. But we didn't just clap—we got up on our feet, cheered, and hugged Tyreece. How had we not known that he possessed such a gift? Ron asked if he knew any other songs, and Tyreece grabbed a djembe drum. (We have them all over our school.) He sat on the floor and sang "The Little Drummer Boy" while pounding every beat on that drum. Not only was Tyreece's voice perfect but his face was radiant. He was alive, and I had never seen him look more at ease. He had a command of the room—a presence that drew us all in immediately.

Tyreece would go on to share his gift many times over the rest of the years that he attended RCA, and he continues to do so as a high school student. He relates to his world through his music and blesses everyone who knows him. I once told Tyreece that I felt like he seemed more comfortable on a stage than anywhere else, and he responded, "Mrs. Bearden, whatever I do with my life, it will have to involve music." I hope that it does, Tyreece, because you have been created with a gift that is meant to be shared.

I could easily list the multiple talents of every student I have taught, but I would not first list things that you might think would be obvious for an English teacher to note, such as the child's writing ability or reading comprehension level. I think of students like Jessie, a girl I taught fourteen years ago, who could light up any room simply by walking into it. Her joy and her radiance were contagious, and I could feel her presence before I even saw her. And then I realize how Dasia and Adejah possess that same amazing gift. I think of Shepard, who could hold her own with any boy on any court, and how she had a gift for being both feminine and strong, just like Aujahuna, D'Nai, and Daryl Ann after her. I love the sweet spirit that Stephanie brought to my class ten years ago, and I found that same kind heart in Regan, Natasha, and Natalie. I give thanks for the character of young men like Tessema and Malachi—boys who will one day be extraordinary family men. I smile whenever I think of the humor that Osei, Jordan, and Jai brought to every situation. And I recognize the natural leaders, like Brenton, Brandon, and Julian—who I believe will one day make a great difference in the world. How can I identify these gifts? It is easy because every single child on this planet has his or her own set of talents, and each is extraordinary in his or her own way.

This all came to light for me one night when my daughter Madison and I put together a jigsaw puzzle. As we laid each piece out on the table, I thought about how every piece was jagged, misshaped, and even ugly when studied in isolation. However, as the picture began to take shape, I thought about how every piece had its own purpose and place. When each piece was placed where it belonged, it became a beautiful, integral part of the big picture, and its flaws were much less visible.

We are like those puzzle pieces; each of us is uniquely created to be a part of a bigger picture where we can bring beauty to the world around us. None of us is perfect, but when we find where we fit, our sense of purpose begins to take shape. Often the biggest problem is that we are trying to fit into the wrong place or to connect to another piece that isn't meant for us. Some us of don't even get started making the puzzle—we are still rattling around in our boxes, afraid to see the wonder that we can help to create. We must seek to nurture our gifts and use them to their fullest. There is no one on the planet exactly like you. Each of us is a one-of-a-kind limited edition.

When we moved into our former house, I was excited by the fact that it sat adjacent to our local YMCA and several soccer fields. On crisp autumn Saturday mornings, I loved to lie in bed with the windows open and listen to the sounds of children laughing and crowds cheering them on as the youth soccer games took place. I couldn't wait for my daughter Madison to join a team.

As soon as she turned six years old, I signed her up for her first season. She, too, was so very excited, especially about the uniform. On the day of the first game, I invited my parents and my brothers to attend—they needed to witness her first moment as a child soccer prodigy.

Imagine my dismay when Madison spent the whole game in the backfield doing cartwheels while the rest of the team went for the ball. It got even worse when she actually sat down and started picking dandelions. All we could do was laugh. She had no interest in that soccer game. Or the ensuing tennis or ballet classes. None of those things captured her passion or her attention, so she happily floated from one activity to the next, blissfully unfazed by the spirit of competition that each required.

Quite honestly, Madison was happiest with a box of crayons, paper, and paint—this would occupy her for hours. And when I did sign her up for her first art lessons, she absolutely loved them. It was art that captured Madison's attention, and through it, she expressed her unique design.

I must admit that I had my expectations for my daughter's life all mapped out: she would make straight A's in high school, receive a scholarship for college, attend the University of Georgia (my alma mater), and graduate magna cum laude. From there, she would attend a graduate school to prepare for a career that would make both a difference and a good salary. Isn't this what all parents would want for their children?

The problem with this is that it was my path for her life,

not hers. Nowhere did my plan address what would make her happy or fulfilled, because in my mind, how could such a plan *not* make her happy?

So, I was more than a little thrown when she didn't have the same all-consuming obsession with grades that I have. I just didn't get how my own child could be wired so differently. In fact, it took a lot of parenting on my part—scheduled, structured homework times, signed agendas, reading together, and consequences for failure to comply—when she went to middle and high school. However, I somehow managed to find a good balance of rewards and consequences and give-and-take. These boundaries were necessary for her, and they helped her develop responsibility. When she went to college, I was proud of this wonderful young lady who knew the importance of hard work. My work was done. Mission accomplished—or so I thought.

Over the course of two years of different conversations and changing majors, it became apparent that Madison felt lost when it came to deciding on the path she should take with her life. In fact, she told me she felt like she was living someone else's life, not her own. She needed something different—something that would celebrate her artistic talent.

Over spring break, Madison sat me down in the most mature of ways and shared that she would like to attend a very reputable cosmetology institute to get her license to style hair. My first thought: *Yeah, right. Noooo way. It's graduate school for you, my child.* But after many conversations, a few arguments, and some tears, I assumed that this was a phase she had to go through and since she was twenty-one years of age, I had to let her follow her path.

I am fully aware that by sharing this, many of you are thinking this: *If Kim was paying for college, then she should have insisted that her daughter finish what she had started. Kim should have put her foot down. If Kim is this so-called great teacher, then her child should have longed to get those degrees.* I hear you. I had those internal conversations, too, and they kept me awake at night.

However, I was wrong, and Madison was right. She graduated from cosmetology school at the top of her class and is a rising star at a major, upscale salon in Atlanta. Not only does she love her career, but she is good at it. Why? Whenever she talks about her work, her eyes light up, her smile widens, and she enthusiastically shares story after story about her experiences. Madison has learned the value of success and of failure, and she is stronger for it. She is young and her journey is just beginning, but for now, she knows what direction she wants to take, and she plans to make a difference in the lives of others.

We all have unique talents and gifts that we are meant to share with the world—we just have to be open to discovering them. If you haven't found your unique gifts or talents, perhaps you are looking in the wrong places. Think of all the qualities you possess that are good, noble, or true. You might not be able to cook gourmet meals, slam-dunk a basketball, or understand physics, but you might be able to support others in times of need or bring laughter to any situation. You may be unable to be a runway model, but you might be able to organize volunteers better than anyone else.

You can have an impact on others that you might not have realized simply because you are choosing to focus on things that you think you *can't* do instead of the things that you *can* do. You are enough. Forget your failures, forget your inadequacies—focus on the gifts that you do have and how you can choose to use them to the fullest. You have something to offer this world. You, my friend, are fearfully and wonderfully made.

CLASS NOTES

- We are all designed with a unique set of gifts and talents.
- Gifts come in many different forms; one doesn't have to be a singer, dancer, or pro athlete to have talents that bring significance to the world.
- Understand that children are all uniquely designed, too, and we must let them explore their gifts.
- Focus on the things that you can do, not the things that you cannot do.
- Understand that you have abilities that can make the world a better place.

HOMEWORK
---

1. Make a list of all of your child's gifts. Try to focus not only on the obvious; think about your child's ability to do things like make others laugh, to show love, or to give freely. Embrace your child's unique abilities and find ways to celebrate them.
2. Make a list of your talents, too. If you struggle with this, ask a trusted friend to provide insight into the qualities that they think are your strengths. Next, reflect upon how you are using these gifts every day.
3. Find ways to use your talents to uplift others through your work, relationships, or volunteerism. The more you utilize your gifts, the happier you will be.

7

OPTIMISM

┌─────────────── COURSE DESCRIPTION ───────────────┐
│ In this class, you will learn the importance of spreading │
│ your own sunshine. │
└───┘

I entered Mr. Clark's math class to find the students still hard at work on a complex problem. The last step required them to add several positive and negative integers.

Leaping on the desk, Mr. Clark exclaimed, "Okay, kids, we are almost done! Now, we have negative thirty-seven plus fourteen. Number thirty-seven will pull. Help me pull!"

"Argh!" the students shouted while pulling an imaginary rope.

"Next fourteen will pull," Mr. Clark continued.

"Argh!" the students joined in again while pulling the imaginary rope in the other direction.

"Now thirty-seven will gobble up fourteen! Gobble with me!" he shouted while eating the imaginary number.

The students followed suit, pretending to eat the imaginary 14 that floated in the air above them.

Mr. Clark went on, "And the answer will be?"

"Negative twenty-three!" they shouted in unison.

"MacKenzy, how do you know?" he asked.

"Because when the positives and negatives fight, you take the sign of the larger number. This time the negative wins."

As her classmates applauded and finished the problem, it struck me that the same thing happens in life. There is a battle between the negative and the positive, and sometimes those negative folks do everything they can to pull down those who have a positive spirit. Like those darn Dementors in Harry Potter, those negative folks can suck your soul right out of you. And my friend, if there is one thing that I know about negative people, it is that misery loves company. Negative people love to recruit. These misery evangelists are working hard to bring others into their fold, so we must work even harder to spread our gospel of positivity. In other words, we have to gobble them up.

I have been blessed to teach many positive students, but Dasia and Zharia are two who definitely belong in the Positivity Hall of Fame. No matter where or what the circumstances, these two girls always see the bright side of every situation, and it is contagious.

During the 2008 elections, RCA students received a tremendous amount of media attention due to a nonpartisan song that they wrote, "You Can Vote However You Like," which encouraged voters to know the issues and go to the polls. The

song became a viral hit on YouTube, and our students performed on CNN, *Good Morning America*, Fox News, and more.
They were even chosen as *ABC World News Tonight*'s Persons
of the Week. Ron beautifully chronicles the story in his own
book, so I will just emphasize that our students stunned and
amazed the country with their knowledge of politics, and they
inspired many. Probably one of the most thrilling experiences
the students had was performing on BET's *106 & Park*.

For those of you who don't know, performing on *106 & Park*
is one of the most exciting things any kid could ever hope to do,
and our students were seriously pumped. The show has a video
countdown format with live musical guests, and Keyshia Cole
and Brandy were scheduled for our day. Right before the show
began its live broadcast, about two hundred audience members
filled the bleachers—many had been waiting outside for hours
just to get into the studio. Most of the guests were attractive
African Americans in their late teens and early twenties, and
it was obvious that those who were chosen to be there oozed
style. My students felt so special because they were given
prime seating right near the stage—a place where they would
appear on camera often.

I have never felt less cool in my life. Not only did I stand
out because I was the only blond, white woman there; I mainly
stood out because I was *old*. As they warmed up the audience,
I could see staff with earpieces giving directions to the multiple cameramen. There were two cameras with ten-foot folding
arms that moved like robots throughout the crowd to get the
right camera angles of the audience's responses. I watched
the arm go over me, under me, and around me—the crew was

going to incredibly great lengths to get our kids on camera but to avoid filming me. Let's face it—a forty-three-year-old white chick in the audience of *106 & Park* looked awkward and almost desperate on my part!

Zharia, always so sweet, looked over her shoulder and said, "You are cool to us, Ms. Bearden!" as she followed her classmates to perform live on camera. I was so proud of their performance—the crowd gave them thunderous applause, and the kids simply beamed. The students were interviewed live by the hosts, Terrence J. and Rocsi, and they spoke eloquently about the need to go out and vote. After they returned to our seating area, the students were giddy to see Keyshia Cole interviewed just feet in front of them.

Finally, Brandy took to the main stage to perform. The crowd was encouraged to rush to the stage to see the live performance up close, and as my students sprang to their feet, I did my best to hang back. I was doing my darnedest to be invisible, but I am afraid I was failing miserably. But suddenly, I felt Zharia's hand in mine, and she and Dasia pulled me with them—right up to the edge of the stage. As Brandy began to sing her new single, the crowd cheered and danced, and I was right there with them. My kids did not care that I was a little out of place—they wanted me right there to share in the joy of the experience with them. And instead of being insecure, hurt, or indignant, I got a kick out of the whole thing. I embraced that I was old, unhip, and unable to dance and just allowed myself to bask in the moment. Thanks to Dasia and Zharia, we laughed, we bobbed, and we had a beautiful time together. Nothing could take that joy away from us—not even the possibility of looking ridiculous while appearing on national television.

Let me give you another example of Zharia's sunshine. After returning from Christmas break, I asked Zharia if her vacation had been enjoyable.

"Mrs. Bearden, we had quite the adventure!" she said smiling.

"Oh, really? What happened?" I asked.

"Well, my whole family was driving through Alabama to see my relatives on Christmas Eve when our car broke down in the middle of nowhere."

"Oh, no!" I exclaimed.

"Yes, and it gets funnier. So there was nowhere to get it fixed on Christmas Eve in this small town, so we had to walk to this creepy little motel. We had to all stay there in one room until the day after Christmas so that we could get it fixed."

"So all five of you stayed in a motel room for Christmas?" I asked sympathetically.

"Yes," she said. "Isn't that hilarious?"

"I am so sorry, Zharia!" I said.

"Mrs. Bearden, there was no reason to be sorry. I got to be with my whole family on Christmas. It was great."

And so is Zharia. Do you know how many teenagers would have been impossible brats in this kind of a situation? There is something truly special about that child. If we could all be more positive like Zharia, imagine how we could affect the outcome of many of life's challenges.

For the past six years, our fifth-grade students have been granted a trip to New York City, thanks to the support of our generous sponsors. The highlight of the occasion is always our own version of *The Amazing Race*. Students are divided into teams of three or four with a chaperone, and they must journey across the city completing physical and intellectual challenges, such as running across the Brooklyn Bridge, unlocking clues at St. Patrick's Cathedral, performing a ballroom dance step in Times Square, conquering a game at Nintendo World, climbing rock walls, mastering subway maps, and finding hidden treasures in Chinatown. Ron is always in a central location. Once one mission is completed, each team texts Ron for the next clue. The day is always educational, exhilarating, and highly competitive.

This particular year, all nine teams had raced all over the city for close to eight hours, and the final challenge was to find answers to several questions at the Intrepid Sea, Air & Space Museum, located at the Chelsea Piers. There were three teams trailing mine closely, but we refused to go down easily. My students—Adejah, Michael, Darius, and Jordan—were tough competitors. We ran to most locations and rarely took the subways, which kept us in the lead for several hours.

As we left the museum, our final clue told us that the first team to arrive at the Dave and Buster's restaurant in Times Square would win the race! We set off on foot while reading the rest of Ron's message; we were told that it would be easiest to grab a bus at a specified station. We ran to the station to wait, but we were dismayed when two other teams caught up to us, and still there was no bus. No cabs were in sight, either. We couldn't bear to lose our lead, so my team decided to discuss the situation. Michael, who is quite the athlete, said, "Guys, we've been running all day. We can do this. I say we go for it!"

Adejah looked at the map and said, "It's really, really far, and there is not really a subway route to get us there any faster. But why not at least try?"

To which Darius added, "I'm up for it. Jordan?"

Jordan could only nod—her asthma had been getting to her. I was a little worried about her, but she said she was game, so we set off on foot. The other two teams had lost their enthusiasm. They hollered that we were crazy, and we just waved as we left them there.

Not long after we rounded the corner, Jordan started to really struggle. The kids stopped to support her. I was proud of the fact that although we had been competing fiercely all day, they still knew that Jordan's well-being was the most important thing, and they told her we could wait or find a cab if she couldn't make it. We sat on a bench while Jordan regained her steady breathing, and I knew that there was no way I was going to let her run again. They complimented one another on how excellently they had performed. Adejah, Darius, and Michael told Jordan that it was okay—no matter what place they came in, they had given 110 percent.

The moment was beautiful, but I simply could not let it be the way the day ended—not after how hard they had worked and how positive they had remained. So, I did what I had to do.

"Jordan, climb on my back."

"Mrs. Bearden, you can't carry me all the way!"

"Just watch me!" I exclaimed as I hoisted her up and started to jog. And so I ran 1.3 miles with Jordan still on my back. Some say it was two miles, some say three; let it be known here that it was 1.3, fueled by the desire to be a positive force for my students, just as they had been positive for me.

We did cross that finish line first, and it was a remarkable day. Just imagine the ripple effect that you can create when your positive actions and energy outweigh your negative responses. Remember—when adding integers, you must take the sign of the larger number. Are positives or negatives the answers to your problems?

OPTIMISM

CLASS NOTES

- Life is full of positives and negatives. We have to work especially hard to gobble up the negatives.
- Positive and negative thinking are both contagious. Be careful what you spread.
- If we learn to look at life through a positive lens, we will experience more joy.
- It is up to us to set the tone.

HOMEWORK

1. Check the amount of time you spend complaining. Keep a tally of your negative comments for a couple of days to honestly assess the type of energy you are spreading.
2. Whenever someone makes a negative comment, try to follow up with something positive to say. Don't be argumentative; just point out ways that the glass is half full, not empty.
3. When something goes wrong, try to think of what is going right for you.

8

LOVE

===== COURSE DESCRIPTION =====
In this course, you will learn to love your kids,
unconditionally and in your own way.

When my daughter Madison decided to join the Brownies, I encouraged her wholeheartedly. I bought her the required chocolate-brown vest, and she sparkled with pride whenever she earned a patch. However, I made the mistake of assuming that you could simply iron the patches onto the vest and that would be it, while the other moms would iron *and* sew them to make sure that the patches were perfect and secure. (I found this out the hard way when Madison came home from school with three of her patches hanging by one corner.) This was when we realized that the other moms were ultraorganized and ultraenthusiastic. They were all-around Ultra-Moms. They created meeting calendars, snack calendars, craft calendars, and more. I so wanted to be like they were, but juggling motherhood and teaching often left me scrambling for time. They seemed to handle organizing life with such ease, and I was intimidated by their ability to do it all so well.

I was teaching one day when I received a message from a troop mom about the pudding cups that I was supposed to send for snack that day. What? Today was my snack day? How had I missed that? During my planning period I ran to the principal's office and begged for mercy. She allowed me to rush to the store, where I filled my cart with double the amount of required pudding, and I probably broke a few traffic laws on my way to the library where the meeting was held. I darted in, handed over the bags, and kissed my daughter as I ran back to my car. I couldn't be late for a parent conference at three thirty back at my own school.

When I returned to the library to pick Madison up at the end of the meeting, the troop's leader was in the middle of an animated conversation with three other moms. They abruptly stopped talking as I approached and gave me *the look*: they stared at my face and then slowly scanned their eyes down my body to my shoes and then back up again. At that moment, I felt like I was standing before the head cheerleader in high school while the rest of the squad assessed me, and I was *definitely* not going to be asked to join the team.

The Super Ultra-Mom smiled at me and smugly trilled, "Didn't you get my message? I needed it to be *chocolate* pudding. We were making 'dirt' for our craft and snack today, and you sent vanilla pudding. We couldn't do a craft because it wouldn't work with vanilla!" As she reprimanded me, the Ultra-Moms shook their heads in disappointment. I apologized, while my face and neck burned and I tried to swallow the huge lump in my throat. I allowed this woman to make me feel guilty and inadequate. I was only rescued when Madison came running over and jumped into my arms. My sadness slowly started to subside.

As we drove home, I was very quiet. Perhaps my seven-year-old daughter perceived my mood, or maybe it was just divine timing, but she looked at me and said, "Mim, I am so glad that you are my mom."

"Really? Why do you say that, sweetie?"

"Because you are a good person and you help lots of people all the time. Today in circle time we talked about heroes, and I talked about you. I told my troop how we painted sheets to look like other planets for your classroom last weekend and how much fun we had. I told everyone about you and what a good teacher you are and that everybody wishes that they could have a teacher just like you."

The tears I'd been holding back now started to spill down my cheeks. I started to giggle uncontrollably. Madison began to giggle, too, and we laughed and talked the rest of the way home. My daughter didn't care about pudding cups or the crooked badges on her vest. She only wanted a mom who loves her. I felt immediately better.

This situation made me realize that we often go through life measuring ourselves against unrealistic standards. I run a school, teach full-time, and have a family—I even have pets. I have been a single, working mom, and I know the challenge of trying to be everything to everyone. And you know what? It is okay if we order takeout. It is okay if the Christmas cards are late; it is even okay if that area behind the dryer is growing dust bunnies. Moms don't have to do everything perfectly. In fact, when we pamper our kids, we often cripple them from learning how to be self-sufficient. I have known parents who write their children's papers, do their projects, tell them how to think, and hover over their children's lives to make sure they never stumble. When these kids trip, they don't know how to pick themselves up, dust themselves off, and move on. They do not know how to make choices, learn from mistakes, or handle conflict on their own. There is a delicate balance of leading children and allowing them to walk forward alone—they must have the opportunity to navigate through life's twists and turns. We can't let them go too far off where they will get injured, but an occasional fall or branch in the face can be good for them!

I once taught two beautiful, bright, creative, and independent-minded twin girls named Mariah and Maleigha. Their mom, Mrs. Cooper, is pretty amazing, too. She runs a preschool, raises six kids, and still manages to look like a million bucks whenever I see her. When her daughters were in the fifth grade, she sent me this email:

LOVE

Dear Mrs. Bearden,

Not sure if you all received the memo, but obviously 5th graders are the smartest kids in the world and they don't need any help or guidance from others. Well, at least that is what my 5th graders have so graciously told my husband and me. We have tried endlessly to assist them with creating and implementing systems to help them become more organized or just to assist with homework.

Yet, they have basically said they are frustrated with us because we don't think like them and they can figure things out for themselves. Soooooooooooooooooooooo, we have decided to take their advice and let them do everything themselves. For the next couple of weeks, we are not assisting them at all. They are on their own! I am not pushing them to read, study notes, iron clothes, ensure they have on proper attire, etc. We just wanted you all to know what was going on just in case you began to see a drop in grades like we have over the past couple of weeks (which ironically is when we began stepping back).

This is really hard for me as a parent because my daughters have never received anything other than A's on their report cards! But sometimes a little tough love is what it is going to take to get through. Thanks again for everything. Who knows? Maybe this will even empower them!

I think Mrs. Cooper is brilliant. Over the next few weeks, the girls' grades did drop slightly, and they did fall apart a little, but they were able to learn an important life lesson on their own. By stepping back and allowing them to falter, Mrs.

Cooper was showing her tremendous love for her daughters by being the very best of guides. The girls learned what they should do on their own, but they also learned the importance of needing support as they move forward on their individual paths. Both girls are now thriving.

If you are able to whip up gourmet dinners and keep an immaculate house, you truly have my undying awe and respect. But even if you can't, it is okay. As long as the greatest investment in your home is the love that you create and spread, you, my friend, have succeeded in my eyes.

CLASS NOTES

- If you feel inadequate at home, you are not alone. Most of us feel that way sometimes.
- Release the guilt and stop thinking that you have to be like others to be a good spouse or parent.
- Realize that when we do everything for our children, we keep them from learning how to take care of themselves.
- It is good to show tough love by allowing our children to stumble at times.
- When we focus on building a home with love, everything else is secondary.

HOMEWORK

1. Make a list of the things that you would love for your children to say about you. Would you prefer for them to say that you mop well or that you play with them? Prioritize your time around the things that will yield the greatest return with your family.
2. If your house is truly out of control, set aside a weekend to get organized so that you can better function and release the guilt. Get rid of things you don't need and straighten things so that you are able to operate more efficiently.
3. Assess your involvement with your child's life. Are you there to support and guide them, or are you doing everything for him/her? Hint: if you are spending your night completing your child's homework or writing lengthy emails each night to your eight-year-old child's coach, you might be a helicopter parent.

4. Want to know how you are really doing as a member of your family? Have a family discussion and ask for honest feedback. Be willing to receive it without being defensive, and find ways to focus on the things that your family values the most. Elicit their help with tasks you must complete.

9

GENEROSITY

================ COURSE DESCRIPTION ================
In this course, you will learn how lifting others can help lift yourself.

The eighth-grade girls entered the front door of RCA as sooth-
ing music filled the lobby. I greeted them at the check-in table.
"Hello. Welcome to Spa RCA. Do you ladies have an appointment for tonight?"

"Why, yes, ma'am, we do," Robin said, playing along.

"Wonderful. Please have a seat in our lobby, and one of our
technicians will be with you shortly." I waited for all of the paja-
ma-clad girls to arrive before I paged the "technicians"—our
female staff members—and we ushered them up the stairs.

It was our annual Girls' Night, a tradition for our eighth-
grade girls. In the past, we had taken the girls to a play, but two

of our most insightful teachers, Mrs. Barnes and Dr. Jones, had decided that this year's event would be a special spa night so that we could better spend quality time with each girl.

When we arrived in the loft upstairs, Mrs. Coss served a spread that was worthy of the spa at the Ritz, complete with white linen tablecloths and fresh-cut flowers. We feasted on cucumber sandwiches, chicken salad, fresh lemonade, and an assortment of treats while chatting and catching up on the girls' lives. Bellies full, the girls entered my classroom, which had now been completely transformed.

Crisp white sheets covered every surface, and piano music permeated the massive room. Spa stations lined the walls, and after a local beautician gave a passionate speech on inner beauty as well as hair care, we began our special ceremony.

One at a time, female staff members stood up to declare what made each of the girls unique. Each girl was assigned a color that represented her personality and spirit, and the staff members gave the girls customized spa baskets, filled with items in each girl's assigned color. As I gave Adejah her silver basket, I told her the many ways that she radiated goodness. Her smile and hug warmed my heart.

Then we broke the group into trios for their spa rotations. The girls were treated to nail painting, toe painting, shoulder massages, and hand massages, all executed with love and care from their female teachers and staff. We chatted with the girls about school, friendships, boys, their beauty, and their character. We pampered them, we comforted them, and we made each feel valued.

At the end of the night we sat in a circle, and the girls

expressed their appreciation. Some shared how they had had difficult summers; there were stories of divorce and family struggles, loss and personal challenges. As the girls reminisced about the evening, Ariana and Michaela said it had been the best night of their whole summer, and Alexis and Natasha thanked us for showing us how much we love them. Jordan commented on how fortunate they are to have female staff whom they can go to if ever they need anything, and the girls all hugged us and thanked us profusely before departing.

Every little girl needs to feel beautiful, comforted, valued, and cherished. By serving them, we elevated their perceptions of themselves. There is nothing more honorable than serving a child with unconditional love. That spa night took a lot of teamwork and effort, but it was worth it. The more you uplift others, the stronger you become. In fact, your power to uplift others is exponentially increased.

When Ron and I created the school, we had dreams of making it into a premier educational institution—one that would train other teachers and would promote creativity, innovation, passion, and rigor while teaching the importance of manners and respect. On the night of our first graduation in June 2010, I realized that our dreams had come true, yet even we had been somewhat shortsighted. Why? When we set our goals, we hadn't yet met our special first group of graduates. Over the course of three years, these students had not only affected people in the city of Atlanta, they had inspired individuals across the country and around the world.

When this small group of students graduated, they had earned almost $1 million in scholarships . . . *for high school.*

They had been featured on CNN, *Good Morning America,* FOX News, *NBC Nightly News,* BET, and countless other national programs. *World News Tonight* had even named them their Persons of the Week for their song encouraging others to vote during the presidential election. They had performed at the U.S. Capitol for the first lady. They had helped us create the spirit and heart of RCA, and their test scores were exemplary.

All of these things were impressive, but what made me most proud was the way that they truly embraced how we had taught them the importance of serving others.

For example, I took a group of twelve of these students out to lunch one afternoon on the way home from a local field trip. We ate at a well-known restaurant in Atlanta, one that had been open for many years. The kids fawned all over our sweet waitress. They were polite and well-mannered, and they were grateful for the lunch and the service. As we left the restaurant, each of the students spontaneously hugged the waitress, thanked her, and wished her a wonderful day. I made one last circle around the table to make sure we hadn't left a mess, and the waitress approached me with tears in her eyes. She then told me that in thirty years of waiting tables, no one had ever made her feel as significant or appreciated as our students did. That, my friends, is power.

Every year for the past six years, we have been fortunate to take our students to Nevada to visit a ranch owned by some of RCA's very special supporters—Tom and Alicia Maxey. The Maxeys and Delta Air Lines generously sponsor this opportunity, and our students love learning how to ride horses, herd cattle, and care for the animals. The ranch is located about three hours from the nearest city, and the cowboys who work it lead somewhat isolated lives. The cowboys were kind, patient, and all-around wonderful to our kids. They taught them to rope, to ride, and even to dance the Virginia reel.

One of the cowboys was noticeably quiet at first. He was helpful, but he was reticent and seemed almost nervous about working with the kids. I didn't think much about this because many people who don't work with kids often feel the same way. However, on the second day, I noticed that he was now spending more and more time talking to my students and teaching them how to feed and care for the animals.

Whenever we take an overnight field trip, we always end each night with circle time, where we share our thoughts about the day's events. It is always a wonderful way to reflect on our experiences. That night, we held circle time with our new cowboy friends. The shy cowboy stood up and spoke to the group. Tears filled his eyes as he thanked the students for making him feel like a part of our family. He shared how the students had been so eager and interested in everything he had to say. He ended with "I never knew . . . ," choking on his tears as he sat down.

It was later that I found out what the end of that sentence was supposed to be. You see, that rough-and-tumble cowboy had never had the opportunity to spend time with an African American before, let alone a group of thirty amazing African-American children. He was overwhelmed by their spirit and their kindness.

Those students left a beautiful legacy behind after they graduated. Our students realize that if they truly want to be powerful leaders, they must gain their strength from supporting others, not pulling them down. And the ripple effect spreads to our families, community, and beyond.

Last Christmas, the RCA parents and students had a wonderful idea: they suggested that we hold a Christmas party for the children in our neighborhood. RCA is located in a zip code where the per capita income is $9,953 a year, so there is obviously a great deal of need in our community. Our students made invitations and delivered them to day-care and community centers, and they each purchased a small gift to give another child. Our parents went to businesses and obtained sponsors, and on a cold, clear December night, our families were ready to spread love and holiday cheer.

The party was to begin at 5 P.M., but by 4 P.M. a line had already formed around our building. As soon as the parents and students were able to complete the setup, we opened the gates to bright-eyed children, many of whom would not receive any other gifts that Christmas. I watched my students, parents, and staff play games, paint faces, blow bubbles, present gifts, and serve homemade food to the guests. We sang Christmas carols in the parking lot as we all joined hands and watched the lighting of our Christmas tree—a tree that we would later give to one of the families to take home. Then the dancing began. Music filled the parking lot as parents, students, staff, and families from the community all danced with abandon. My students picked up little children, twirled them, hugged them, and showed them steps to follow. The joy was contagious; in fact, at the end of the night, my cheeks hurt from smiling so much.

Even if you are experiencing life's lowest points, you have

two choices. You can focus on yourself and all of your pain, or you can choose to focus on encouraging others. The second choice has a far greater healing effect. The key is exposure. The more we genuinely expose ourselves to the plights of others, the more we will understand, respect, and care for them. Over the years, we have sorted coats for the homeless, completed landscaping at community centers and homeless shelters, sung at retirement homes, worked at orphanages, and fed those in need. And each time I watch my students readily help those around them, I am reminded that you never stand stronger than you do when you raise the spirits of those around you.

At our school, we clap and cheer for one another, and we embrace others' good fortunes. We teach our children that we are in this together and that we must help each other find success. Sometimes it is hard; the weighty challenges that some people face can be more than one can handle alone. But together, we can embrace others and let them know that they are valued. The more we elevate one another, the stronger we all become.

CLASS NOTES

- At times, we all need to feel comforted, valued, and cherished.
- Lifting up others has an exponential ripple effect.
- Children should be taught to help others from an early age; they can learn this by watching adults around them do the same.
- When we support others' needs together, we all become stronger.

HOMEWORK

1. Reflect on the last time you made an effort to support another person. How did it feel? How did it empower you? Draw upon that feeling and use it to motivate you to help someone in need of encouragement.

2. Be aware of your actions around children. Do you model a spirit of encouragement and support for others? What changes or improvements can you make?

3. Recognize those whose burdens are too heavy to bear alone. How can you help ease the weight they carry?

10

TENACITY

COURSE DESCRIPTION

In this class, you will learn the value of patience and persistence.

Mark loved heavy metal. From his tousled, long blond hair to his Metallica T-shirts and black boots, he embraced the head-banger persona. But he didn't fool me. I taught Mark in 1988—my second year as a language arts teacher.

It seemed that Mark didn't care at all about school—he often missed homework assignments, and there was definitely a lack of motivation on his part. When working in class, he required constant redirection and he could be a handful. He would do the work if I stood over him and guided him, but as soon as I walked away, he would stare into space again. There was a darkness about Mark, a sadness in his eyes that seemed magnified by his all-black wardrobe. But when I could get him to smile, his mischievous grin lit up the room. So this became my mission—well, in addition to getting him to do his homework and behave.

Mark's sidekick was his fellow rocker, Nate. When the two interacted, I watched the dark veil lift. The boys laughed and whispered about inside jokes, and they became downright silly. Sometimes their behavior did get out of hand, however, and on one such occasion, Mark continued to leave his editing group to try to get Nate's attention. After telling him once to return to his desk, he left again, resulting in my decision to issue him an after-school detention. I promptly filled out the form, signed it, and handed it to Mark.

He stuck it in his mouth and chewed.

Obviously, this kid was looking for a reaction, but I refused to give him one. Instead, I calmly asked, "Did you just eat the detention form?"

He nodded as he struggled to swallow the paper still in his mouth.

So I followed up with "Was it good?"

His eyes watered as he tried not to choke on it.

Although I was still learning how to navigate my effectiveness as an educator, I had figured out the importance of building relationships with my students, and I knew that Mark was searching for someone to validate him. I would often talk to Mark after class about everything from heavy metal to his spiritual beliefs. Mark was searching for someone or something to believe in, and I just wanted him to know that I had faith in him. I would try to get him to explain why he wasn't doing his work, but his response was often just "I don't know." I found this maddening, especially when he would vow to do better and then repeat the same lack of effort. He was a complex kid to figure out and he didn't have it all together when he left my class at the end of that year.

I prayed that I had planted seeds in Mark that would take root and make a difference in his future. I hoped that when he felt that life was meaningless, he would remember the things that we had discussed during our talks. This is what we all must hope for when nurturing children and others whom we affect. Sometimes we never see the fruits of our labors, but even if we don't, we must believe that we planted something good that will one day grow.

In Mark's case, I was blessed to see the outcome—a full twenty-five years later. Mark is now married to an elementary school principal, and he has three beautiful children, whom he adores. He is a wonderful man. And Nate is still Mark's best friend.

And this is why I teach—to plant seeds that will one day help young men and women grow to be their best. Every word, every deed, every outpouring of love has the potential to instill something that will later empower that child and give him or her strength from which to draw. Just as the smallest of seeds can yield the most magnificent trees, so we cannot underestimate the power of the simplest gesture or comment.

About a year ago, I delivered a keynote speech at a school located in a neighboring school district. I always make an effort to connect with my audience and read their expressions, and I couldn't help but notice the eager look of one young teacher.

Throughout my address she nodded, wide-eyed and attentive. When I spoke about the need to love and nurture our students, her eyes pooled with tears. At the end of my talk, the principal hugged me and shared that she had a surprise for me: that young teacher in the audience was Laura, a former student of mine. Although I didn't recognize her at first, as soon as she told me her name, the memories of her came flooding back. Laura then went on to tearfully recount a story that I didn't recall: during a conference with Laura and her mother, I had looked her mother in the eye and said, "I hope that one day my daughter will grow up to be just like your daughter."

Laura went on to tell me, "I never forgot that. When I felt insecure or awkward, I drew on that. I thought that it was the most wonderful thing anyone could ever say about me."

I do remember that Laura was a lovely, caring, and kind child. Gentle and shy, she was often happy to stay out of the spotlight. That one simple sentence that I uttered to her mother planted a seed that remained with her sixteen years later. I am so proud to know that Laura is now a phenomenal English teacher, changing the lives of others.

It is easy for all of us to become discouraged when we feel that we have nurtured a child who doesn't respond to our efforts. It is even more frustrating when we feel like we aren't appreciated for all that we are trying to do to help. But we must cling to the hope that our efforts have made a difference and that one day, that child will draw on the things that we have instilled within them.

I love my daughter, and I love shopping, but when she was in middle school, I certainly did not love shopping *with* my daughter. Madison hit middle school in the midst of the low-low-jeans era. Whenever we went school shopping, I would make Madison sit down in the dressing room so that I could see just what could be seen, and those dressing room memories are far from warm and fuzzy. She would try to debate my decisions and rationalize why she needed certain outfits. When I vetoed something, she acted as if I had shot her. And honestly, the tension left me exhausted and exasperated.

Years later, we exchanged these texts:

Madison: Omg, Mim. I am at Target in the dressing room. There is a middle school girl in here, and she is horrible. Her mother keeps telling her that things are inappropriate, and she is sighing and arguing and acting so disrespectfully. I want to go tell this girl that her mom is right and she is being a brat.
Me: I am having bad flashbacks.
Madison: I know, Mim. That is why I texted. I am so sorry if I ever sounded like that. I hate to think that I ever made you feel like that mom must feel. I love you so much and appreciate you. Thx for teaching me how to be a lady!

If you had approached me in the dressing room during those shopping trips and told me I was planting seeds, I would have argued that I was just putting out fires. But in reality, although Madison didn't readily accept my guidance at the time, it took root and later made a difference. She just required a little pruning and care along the way. We all do.

CLASS NOTES

- We must take the time to plant seeds of goodness, faith, and wisdom within others.
- It is easy to grow discouraged when we do not see the fruits of our labor, but growth takes time.
- Sometimes we don't have the opportunity to see the change, but that does not mean that we didn't instill meaningful values. We can't lose faith that we have made a difference.
- Even the smallest words or deeds can plant seeds that will flourish years later.
- We must make sure that we are instilling positive messages that will yield positive results.

HOMEWORK

1. Embrace opportunities to follow up with former students or mentees to see how they are doing. Celebrate and acknowledge their accomplishments, no matter how big or small.
2. Take time to meet with former students or mentees and ask for suggestions for how you can do a better job of "seed planting" in the future.
3. Be intentional with your comments, compliments, and suggestions for growth.
4. Remain patient when working to help children, and do not grow weary or frustrated if they do not respond in the way that you hope they will. Believe that one day, the seeds will take root and grow.

11

INSIGHT

┌─────────────── COURSE DESCRIPTION ───────────────┐
In this course, you will learn the importance
of celebrating differences.
└───┘

It had been a long day. Six of my students and I had been traveling since early that morning—we were visiting a top boarding school in the Northeast, where they had been invited to interview for academic scholarships. We were staying at a hotel located one mile from the campus—it was recommended to all of the scholarship hopefuls. As we dragged ourselves into the lobby, I was proud that my students, despite their exhaustion, still approached the check-in desk with a smile and good manners. The three boys and three girls graciously thanked the clerk for their keys and walked over to retrieve their bags.

As he handed me the key, the clerk said, "What sport do they play?"

"Excuse me?" I asked.

"What sport?" he asked more slowly.

"Sport? Well, a couple of them play sports. Why?" I asked.

"Well, aren't they here because they are a sports team?" he asked.

And then I understood; it seemed that he had drawn this conclusion since these students were African American. I responded, "They are here because they are brilliant scholars who will be interviewing for academic scholarships. They are all being heavily recruited—for their academic accomplishments," I said. As I said it, the students turned to hear the conversation.

"Oh, um, I just assumed they were a sports team. Okay, um, well, have a nice night," he said.

I was fuming.

"It is okay, Mrs. Bearden," said Rashad. "It happens all the time."

Jordan added, "People just assume we only play sports. I love playing football, but there is more to me than that."

Yes, Jordan, there is. All six of those students went on to receive academic scholarships to some of the top high schools in the country.

Did that clerk mean any harm by his comments? Probably not. But they were made out of ignorance. And it has happened on more than one occasion. I have been with my students when they are all dressed in suits and ties, walking quietly through a public place, only to be asked that same question about whether they're on an athletic team. It doesn't matter if I have a mixture of fifth- and eighth-grade students, boys and girls. I can't think of a single organized sports team that has ten-year-old girls and fourteen-year-old boys playing together, but I still get the question. However, this never happened once in the twenty years that I taught groups of predominantly white children. These stereotypes bother my students, and they have told me so. "Mrs. Bearden, we love sports and lots of us play them, but they shouldn't just assume we are a sports team just because we are African American."

"I agree. How do you think we should respond?"

Jordan replied, "That we are scholars." The students all nodded in agreement. And so that is what my kids will tell you. They are brilliant and talented scholars who also might happen to be able to play sports, sing, dance, and spread joy and awareness to those who still only look at the world through one set of binoculars.

As a white, middle-aged woman from suburbia, I have learned a great deal about humanity from working at the Ron Clark Academy. In my lifetime, I have met and formed relationships with many individuals who have inspired me and helped mold me into the person who I am, but they, for the most part, were very much like me. My life lacked another dimension, like a melody without harmony. I lacked the depth that can only be gained by expanding my circle and seeing the world through the eyes of different peoples.

At RCA, we say that *we do see color*. We believe that if you don't see color, you don't see culture. We see color, but we embrace it, we celebrate it, and we seek to understand the world from others' perspectives. We have many similarities, but we also have differences. We talk about race often because we have found that many adults in our country don't know how to talk about it. We aim to help raise a generation of students who can have the discussions that need to be had so that our country will be a healthier, more unified place.

We teach our students that they are not only the descendants of slaves; they are the descendants of African kings and queens and great peoples with a rich history. It is through this philosophy that my world has been enhanced and enlightened. I have learned about the ugliness of racism and the other inequities that still exist in this world—I have now witnessed and seen it firsthand, and it breaks my heart. My parents always taught me to love all people, so I grew up with a worldview where I assumed that most people see things the way that I do. I now know that this isn't the case, and it breaks my heart.

As a young, white girl who grew up in suburbia, I never had a conversation with anyone about what it meant to be a white girl—I just was one. However, I have learned that my African-American students usually need to have many family discussions about what it is to be black and how this will affect their reality. How they shop, how they approach people, how they drive—all of these situations can lead to difficulties if they are not careful.

My staff, students, and I have had frank conversations about our cultural similarities and differences, but we can do this because we have developed a safe environment where we respect and want to learn from one another. Cultivate relationships with individuals from different races, ethnicities, political parties, religions, and viewpoints. Talk with them about how you are different and how you are alike. And most important, listen. You might learn something about your world that you never realized before.

CRASH COURSE

---------------------------- CLASS NOTES ----------------------------

- Racism is still alive in our country and our world.
- We must seek to understand the cultural and ethnic backgrounds of others.
- We need to raise a generation of students who can have meaningful discussions about race.
- When we expand our circle to include friends who are different than we, our life is greatly enhanced.

---------------------------- HOMEWORK ----------------------------

1. Seek out relationships with those who are different than you, and begin the conversation about race. Be open-minded. Listen. And learn.
2. Do not make the assumption that you know what it is like to walk in another person's shoes. Remember this when forming judgments and making comments.
3. Learn your history and the history of other peoples. Teach it to the children in your life.
4. If you harbor feelings of racism toward any group, you must release them. You must change, for your sake as well as the sake of future generations.

12

EXPECTATIONS

COURSE DESCRIPTION

In this course, you will learn the power of setting the bar high and believing in every child's ability to succeed.

When my fifth-grade students and I visited New York City, we took a tour of Harlem to learn more about its rich history, especially during the Harlem Renaissance. As we passed the Apollo Theater on our tour bus, the students asked if they could get out and take a picture. After all, most had watched *Showtime at the Apollo* their whole lives. Smiling enthusiastically, they gathered to take a group photo, but we were saddened to learn that the theater was closed to any tours—there was a rehearsal going on inside.

So, the students took their pictures outside. What we

didn't realize was that we were being watched by one of the employees of the theater, and he was impressed by the polite manner of our students and their joyful dispositions. An elderly man with a spring in his step and a twinkle in his eye, he approached us and asked, "Would you like to come inside for a tour? I have some extra time before the lunch break is over."

Thanking him with hugs, we joined him for an impromptu private tour of the building. Then he took us into the theater. We eagerly accepted his invitation to sit in the famous red seats. As we stared at the intricately carved woodwork on the balconies and surrounding the stage, our guide was joined by several other employees who had been hanging out in the back of the theater, and together they told us about all of the incredible greats who had sung in that very place. My students sat on the edges of their seats, rapt with attention. And then, an employee asked if anyone would like to sing.

Aleyna, our own little songbird, took to the stage with the poise and soul of a jazz great, and she serenaded us with "Sista" from The Color Purple. As she sang, her voice rang throughout the theater, and to us, she was a legend. And by the look on her face, she could see the belief in our eyes—she echoed it as she sang with all her heart and soul. She saw greatness in herself because we saw it in her. We all stood and cheered wildly as she joyfully walked across the stage and rubbed the stump of the Tree of Hope, a tradition at the Apollo, before departing.

Every child deserves a moment like this one, where he or she feels celebrated. A moment where others comprehend that child's limitless potential and predict that there will be success in their future. Every adult needs such a moment, too.

We strive to give these kinds of experiences to our students and tell them about the gifts we see inside of them, and we tell them this often. At times, we thrust them into the spotlight, requiring them to step out and share their gifts with the world. Our students know that to us, no child is invisible.

Recently a film crew visited our school to interview my teachers, and the amazing Mrs. Barnes, my fellow English teacher, was asked, "What would you like for all teachers to know?"

I loved her answer: "Every child wants to be seen."

Isn't that true for all of us? Far too many kids hide behind invisibility cloaks every day. Now, I know that some people are shy and don't crave the spotlight—this isn't what I am talking about. In fact, Mrs. Barnes even describes herself as an intro-vert. I'm talking about wanting others to know that you are significant—that you count. We all need to know that we are making contributions to the world.

My staff is full of the most incredible individuals, and three of the most spirited are Mr. Kassa, Mr. Bruner, and Mr. Berna-din. I love that whenever our kids (or our staff) do something well, they shout, "I see you, Symphoni! I see you, Quivion!" What they are really saying is "You are special! You make a dif-ference! You are loved!"

One of my favorite things about RCA is that everybody knows your name—literally. We require all our current stu-dents to memorize the names and faces of all our new students before they ever set foot on our campus for the first time. On the day of our meet-and-greet, we drape our front gates with velvet curtains. When we open them, the students are whisked down a long red carpet while all of our staff, students, and parents cheer their names. These new students are always taken aback, but they are filled with delight as the bigger kids chant their names over and over again in unison. We send a message on that very first day: "You will not be invisible here. You belong; we understand who you are. We *see* you."

Oftentimes, we have to identify the greatness within another before they are able to see it in themselves. When we choose to do this, we have the ability to transform another's perception of self. The summer before we officially opened the doors of the Ron Clark Academy, we received an exciting phone call: we were asked to host a session for the Americas Competitiveness Forum, a convention for government ministers, private-sector leaders, academics, and nongovernmental organizations from thirty-four countries in the Western Hemisphere. The convention was going to be held in Atlanta, and the forum organizers wanted to visit a school that would place an emphasis on a global curriculum. Of course we agreed.

There was one small problem: our school hadn't even opened yet, and renovations on the building wouldn't be complete for a month. In what came to be known as classic RCA style, we jumped into overdrive. We notified our very first of fifth- and sixth-grade classes that they would attend an orientation session at the YMCA, and we met with them every day for a week. In five short days we required them to learn the names and locations of the thirty-four countries in the Western Hemisphere that would have representatives at the event. The students memorized the names of the prime ministers, ministers of education, and government officials. They were taught how to give a firm handshake, look someone in the eye, and hold a conversation, even if it required an interpreter. They learned how to give a tour of RCA while we walked among the construction workers who frantically tried to get the building into shape, and they memorized the bios of every member of the RCA staff. They even prepared a song to perform.

We explained to the students that this would be the unveiling of RCA to the entire world, and so it was the responsibility of all of us to put our best foot forward to show everyone who we are. The kids bonded together beautifully, despite the fact that they were overwhelmed with all the information that they were required to learn. Some of the students immediately emerged as leaders—Kennedy and Travis were given speeches to deliver, and we knew that they would impress all who met them. Others, like Caleb, were more reticent. Caleb was shy and quiet throughout the whole week, but we did our best to encourage him and let him know the importance of carrying himself with confidence. His handshake had been weak and he mumbled his name, so we practiced again and again. Caleb listened with a quiet intensity as he tried to implement everything we taught him, and he politely and respectfully accepted the advice that we gave him. We told him that we believed in him and that we knew that he was ready to show the world the greatness within him.

On the night before the forum, community volunteers and family members helped us hang pictures and install lockers by flashlight since we didn't have power yet. We swept floors, cleaned bathrooms, and assembled desks until the wee hours of the morning. It was a long night, but the energy and excitement in the building were palpable, and we anxiously completed every task with adrenaline-fueled enthusiasm.

On June 12, 2007, the first students of the Ron Clark Academy gathered in the parking lot in their blazers and ties. They looked so sharp that I beamed with pride, despite the fact that butterflies were having a party in my stomach. The Secret Service arrived early to check the premises, and then a motorcade pulled through the gates. As a black stretch limousine arrived bearing U.S. flags, we knew that it must be Carlos Gutierrez, the U.S. secretary of commerce. He had a commanding presence as he stepped out of the vehicle. He turned to smile at our students, and without hesitation, it was Caleb who boldly stepped forward, looked Secretary Gutierrez dead in the eye, firmly shook his hand, and said, "Welcome to the Ron Clark Academy! My name is Caleb, and we are honored to have you here today."

Caleb could have allowed one of his classmates to take the lead, and he could have been a far more timid version of himself. Instead, he chose to show the world the best version of himself—he chose to shine. We had read his story correctly—there was definitely more to this precious child than he had previously shown to others.

Too often, we all look at the context clues around us and use them to make incorrect inferences and draw the wrong conclusions. I believe that every one of us has a story that is still being written, and it is constantly evolving. But to me, the real beauty is this: we have the ability to affect the lives of those we touch; we can have an influence that will help the story progress more positively. Through our belief in others, we can help them believe in themselves and show them how to revise their lives in ways that will help them find true success and fulfillment. Sometimes, it is as simple as exposing our students to something that they thought might be out of reach for them. It was this mind-set that inspired me to transform my classroom into the Bearden Emergency Medical Center.

"Incoming! Doctors, report to your designated OR, stat!" I exclaimed.

As the students, that is, doctors, hurriedly reported to their operating tables, they readied themselves for surgery. Donned in their surgical gloves, masks, and caps, they embraced their roles wholeheartedly. The heart monitors buzzed about them as ambulance sirens signaled their approach. This was a life-or-death situation, for the students would be operating on grammarians who had lost their parts of speech.

White sheets covered every available space, IVs hung from poles, and patient charts lay ready for the surgeons to analyze each problem and determine which transplants would be necessary to save each grammarian's life. Other surgeons worked feverishly to adjust clauses, repair comma splices, and heal grammarians who suffered from acute sentencitis.

As I, the chief surgeon, monitored the situation, I noted that one group of students had acquired poorly imitated German accents. When I inquired, Jordan replied, "Ya, ya. Ve are a group ov specialists who were flown een from Munich just this morning!"

"Dr. Bearden, please report to OR three, stat!" Brandon joked while raising his hand with a question.

"We have a bleeder over here!" exclaimed Shawl.

"My patient's vital signs are low!" interjected Stephanie.

"Here, let me help you stabilize him," offered Tyler.

When students made errors, "blood transfusions" and Band-Aids were applied with great care. Doctors continuously diagnosed problems, performed procedures, and wrote prescriptions for each patient's full recovery.

When the hour was up, it was almost impossible to get the students to leave. Joseph and Zyan said, "Can't we stay here all day, Mrs. Bearden? We have more surgery to do!"

As Stephanie left, she gave me the biggest of hugs. Later she came back and said, "Mrs. Bearden, that was my favorite lesson ever."

"I am so glad, Stephanie. Why was it your favorite?" I asked.

"Well, I want to be a doctor when I grow up. I always play it at home, but when we did it in class, it seemed so real. Now I can actually *see* myself becoming a surgeon one day."

When you look at others around you, do you jump to the wrong conclusions? Do you make predictions based on your prior biases, or do you allow yourself to see each individual anew? Others can read how you view them. When we perceive children with low expectations, they then think of themselves as lowly. When we look at them with disdain, they grow angry. When we only look at all their actions with disappointment, they only see their failures. When we show others that we can visualize their success, they are better able to visualize it, too.

RCA's graduation ceremony has developed a reputation for being something to behold. Although our school is quite small, a crowd of one thousand gathers each year to join us in celebrating the success of our graduates. Through many contacts, we have been blessed to have many celebrities attend, but hands down, the hit of the evening is always our students' speeches. Our students are not allowed to use notes, and you will never see them hide behind a podium. Instead you see confident, poised, brilliant children sharing their stories.

This was beautifully demonstrated when Osei made his speech as the very first valedictorian of the Ron Clark Academy. Our school is tough. Although we laugh, sing, celebrate, and teach with passion and creativity, we set extremely high expectations for our students, both academically and behaviorally. When Osei took the stage at our very first graduation, he shared many beautiful memories about his time at RCA and what he learned. But he also shared that he had gone through a stage where we "fussed" at him quite a bit. In fact, Osei said that if there were an RCA dictionary, an entire page would be dedicated to "fuss." But he went on to share that *to fuss* means "to show great or excessive concern or affection."

Osei admitted that, for a while, he had lost his passion for learning, and failed to put effort into his work. But his teachers were there to fuss at him and to get him back on track. We wouldn't allow him to be less than he could be, and we were relentless. Keep in mind that he was still making straight A's— he had never received a B. But Osei is gifted, and just because he made straight A's, it didn't mean that he was showing dedication, a strong work ethic, and the thirst for knowledge that we required of him. Osei went on to give a phenomenal commencement speech. At the end, he vowed never to forget the place or the people who had taught him so very much, and he ended by saying, "To fuss is to show great or excessive concern or affection. In other words, to show love."

When we set high expectations for others, we show that we believe in them. Setting low expectations tells a child that you believe that they can't perform; they cannot achieve at a high level. And unfortunately, many of our schools are plagued by cultures of low expectations. We have somehow convinced ourselves that students who have challenges should have things cut in half or made easier for them; however, the world won't cut things in half or expect less. We should not expect less from these children; we should just teach them differently. If we can teach children, especially those who struggle, to have a strong work ethic, then we are better preparing them to succeed in whatever they choose to do in life.

At our school, we enforce the value of a strong work ethic with the RCA letterman's jacket. It is a highly coveted possession. Tom and Alicia Maxey (the same two individuals who take us to their ranch in Nevada) purchase the coats each year for all of our fifth graders, but the students must "earn" them by displaying exemplary work ethic, character, enthusiasm, and discipline. Each Friday, our entire staff votes on whether or not each student is ready to receive the jacket. If a single staff member votes "no," then it isn't given. The standards are high. Because the jacket is so very prestigious, our students work with all their might in hopes that they will be named at the next coat ceremony. Students have been known to sleep in their coats on the day that they receive them because they are so very special to them.

When Keenan entered our fifth-grade class, he wanted that coat—badly. Keenan was a child whose school records were less than stellar before he attended our school. His teacher recommendations labeled him as "difficult, a discipline problem, disruptive, and lazy." His grades matched their evaluations. Keenan's home situation was also difficult—his single mom struggled to make ends meet, and his father had never been present in his life. But when our staff first met Keenan, we instantly loved him. He had a sparkle in his eyes and electricity radiated from his body. His smile lit up the room, and even though I figured he could be a handful, I knew that our school was built for kids like Keenan. On the very first day of orientation, Ron and I ate lunch with him to get to know him better. When I asked him what he thought about attending RCA, he was quite candid.

"I'm excited to be here, especially because my fourth-grade teacher said that you'd never take me."

"She said what?" I asked.

"She said that I wasn't good enough for this school. When I showed her my acceptance letter, she rolled her eyes and just handed it back to me."

My blood boiled. "How did that make you feel?"

He shrugged, "Sad. Afraid that she is right. But I am going to do my best to earn my jacket."

Keenan struggled with his emotions and academics when school began, but we reminded him that this was a fresh start where he could show the world the best version of himself. Our staff continued to push and encourage him. We set the highest of expectations for him; we showered him with both love *and* discipline, the two things that he desperately needed the most. Keenan just needed someone to show him how to channel his creativity and energy in positive ways. We recognized his gifts for public speaking and performing, and we created opportunities for him to share these gifts with others. Soon, when he argued with his peers, he learned to apologize, change his behavior, and move on. When he was acting out of turn, he accepted any consequences that were given to him without attitude. As his academics continued to improve, so did his behavior, his effort, and his contributions to his class.

On a Friday afternoon in late February, the whole school gathered in the lobby. Students lined the stairs and filled every available space.

"It is coat day," Mr. Clark said, and the students cheered.

"This young man has a special spark, a special enthusiasm, that brings light and energy to this school. He is clever, talented, smart, and we have set the highest of expectations for him. Every teacher and staff member in this school sees his potential and his greatness, and today, we honor that. I would like to present this coat to . . . Keenan!"

Keenan burst from crowd and ran to Mr. Clark, throwing his arms around him. Tears streamed down his face as he hugged Mr. Clark and then me. As I held him tightly, I could feel him shaking. The entire school stood and started chanting, "Go, Keenan, go Keenan, go!"

In that moment the trajectory of Keenan's life was altered. He was no longer the student who thought that he wouldn't amount to anything. He was no longer the student who couldn't—he was the student who could. We believed in Keenan, and he knew it. As a result, his light now shines brightly as he continues to grow, mature, and become all that he was designed to be.

EXPECTATIONS

I want every one of my students to shine as brightly as Keenan, and so high expectations are the norm in my class. Sometimes it just takes finding different ways for the students to show what they can do.

The theme from *Cops* blared over my classroom speakers as the visiting educators took their seats. My fifth-grade students, aka the Grammar Police, were in the midst of their cadet training to fulfill their mission "To Correct and Serve."

As the chief of police, I explained the task. "Cadets, we have some violators in our midst. Some have made errors in grammar and punctuation, and it is our job to issue them citations. Our guests have baskets full of sentences. Please patrol the room, and when you interact with a guest, draw a sentence from his or her basket. If the guest has violated a rule, you must write a citation specifying the offense and take the suspect to the appropriate correctional facility.

"Please note the locations of the correctional facilities for the following infractions:

Comma splices
Run-on sentences
Fragments
Verb conjugation errors
Pronoun usage errors
Faulty parallelism

"Once you have taken the offender to the appropriate correctional facility, you must explain the charges and give suggestions for rehabilitation by correcting the violating sentence.

After you have done this, the suspect may be released on his own recognizance. If the violator feels that he has been falsely charged, he or she may go to one of our judges to plead his case. Are you ready, cadets?"

"Yes, ma'am!" they exclaimed as they jumped into action.

The music began again and the Grammar Police, adorned with badges on their chests, patrolled the room, issued citations, and readily escorted the offenders to the appropriate correctional facilities. As Judge Brandon, Jacobi, Stephanie, and Kamryn monitored the proceedings, my cadets performed exemplary public service.

"Ma'am, I am afraid I am going to have to take you in on a comma splice infraction," said Zyan in his most authoritative voice. "It appears that you have joined two independent clauses with only a comma. I need to change that to a semicolon or a comma and a coordinating conjunction." The teacher was stunned.

As I passed Nichcolas, I heard him arresting another teacher. "I see here that you used 'me' instead of 'I' in this sentence. I am afraid that you should have used the nominative case here because the pronoun follows a linking verb and acts as a predicate nominative."

In another part of the room I heard Judge Brandon actually side with the student officer when a teacher accused him of a false arrest. "Ma'am, I'm afraid that his citation is correct. The past perfect form of *swim* is *had swum,* not *had swam.*"

When we debriefed with the teachers about the lesson, the message was the same from all who commented: "I can't believe all that these fifth-grade students know." Another added, "These kids can explain grammar better than my tenth graders." Still another said, "I finally understand comma splices after Kendall explained them to me."

At RCA, we have students of all academic backgrounds—those who have tested as gifted, those who have been labeled as average in the past, and those who have struggled significantly before attending our school. My teachers and I believe that it is our responsibility to find ways to arouse curiosity, spark creativity, and teach with rigor so that all children are expected to learn. It takes effort, but every time I see my students rise to my expectations for them, I am reminded that every bit of the effort is worth it. Teachers who visit my class say that all of my students must be gifted. And you know what? Who cares what their prior school records said. They are all gifted. Each and every one of them.

To be clear, I cannot just set high expectations and just tell my kids to get there on their own. I have to help my students reach the standards that I set. And I have to show them that I, too, am willing to go above and beyond. All of our teachers work in this manner. We show the students that we have the highest of expectations for ourselves, and we constantly push ourselves to be better.

This attitude led my staff to create "The Best Day of School Ever." The challenge: we would design a day of school unlike any other—a day that would forever go down in history as an epic example of what education should be. We wanted the students to understand that learning translates well beyond our classroom walls; the world is our classroom. And so after weeks of planning, our magnificent day became a reality.

As parents pulled into the morning carpool line, they were given a flyer and told to read it after they left. The message:

Surprise! We have kidnapped your children.

The Ron Clark Academy is going on location today, and the city of Atlanta will be our classroom as we embark on the adventure of a lifetime!

The students were whisked onto buses by grade level, and each class period was held at a different venue across the city. I taught my language arts class at WXIA studios, and the students appeared on camera on the news set as they read from the teleprompter and learned green screen technology. Next, the students found themselves on the floor of Philips Arena where Ron held math class; they calculated how to determine the number of seats and how their free-throw averages compared to the Atlanta Hawks'. After that, the students were taken to a cage with elephants at Zoo Atlanta as Mr. Townsel taught them about animal behavior. From there, they went to Spanish at a salsa studio with Ms. Estrada and literature at a television studio, where Ms. Barnes taught them about how setting affects the tone of their writing. Another math class was even held at a local pool hall as Dr. Jones showed the students how geometry and angles are used to make the perfect shot.

Every destination was a surprise, and every moment was filled with passion and a joy for learning. At the end of the day, all of the classes convened on the pitcher's mound at Turner Field, the home of the Atlanta Braves. As Ron recapped the day for the students, he explained that we wanted to show them the best that we could offer; we wanted to give them excellence. He went on to explain that in life, we can settle for a single, a double, or even a triple; however, the true joy comes from those grand slams—those moments when we hit it out of the park. And in doing so, we bring everyone along with us. When we set advanced standards, we see advanced results.

CLASS NOTES

- Everyone deserves a moment where he or she feels appreciated and celebrated.
- We need to remind people that they are not invisible; they have purpose and significance.
- When we see the greatness in others, it allows them to see it in themselves.
- Setting low expectations does not help a struggling child; it might even hinder him or her.
- We must draw positive conclusions and make meaningful predictions for the lives of others.
- We have the ability to shape the stories of our lives and the lives of others.

HOMEWORK

1. Think about the children you influence. What greatness do you see in each of them? Make a list of names, and next to each, write your hopes and dreams for that child. When you interact with that child, try to visualize these aspirations and see them coming true.

2. Learn how to tell others the positive things you see in them, especially those with whom you struggle to connect. Understand that they might be suspicious at first, but the more that you embrace looking for those qualities, the more you start to see others through a different lens.

3. Read your own perceptions of yourself. When you predict your future, do you draw negative conclusions and make pessimistic predictions? Take time to jot down what you would like to see in your future. Make a vision board that contains positive notes, quotes, and pictures that will help you rewrite your story.

13

BONDING

=== COURSE DESCRIPTION ===
In this course, you will learn the importance of surrounding
yourself with individuals that enhance your life.

When my daughter Madison was almost two years old, I was thrilled to learn that I was pregnant again. My love for Madison was so deep that I couldn't even fathom being blessed enough to have a second child, so I took very good care of myself. I had learned a lot from my first pregnancy, and this time I ate even healthier and exercised—I did all of the "right" things to ensure that my precious new baby would be okay.

One Saturday morning, I was sixteen weeks into my pregnancy, and I was very tired and remained in my pajamas later than usual. Madison was playing with her dolls, and I was cleaning up around the house. I reached down to pick up a toy and when I stood back up, the room spun, I saw flashes of white, and I grabbed a chair to keep from falling. It was then that I noticed that my entire white nightgown was covered in blood. I cried out for help. I know that I was taken to the hospital and that friends were called, but I was so very upset that the details in my memory bank are more about a blur of emotions than the sequence of events. Terror, fear, uncertainty, and sorrow filled me as a parade of doctors and nurses came to my side.

The baby is dead.

We have to induce labor.

You will need to deliver it.

We will give you something for the pain.

It could take several hours.

We will call someone in to pray with you.

It's a boy.

My parents, who have always been there for me, were out of the country, and I was scared. My husband at the time called friends who came to pick up Madison and take her home, and I know that I just lay in bed, numb from emotion and the medications that dulled my senses.

A wonderful woman volunteer came to my bedside and prayed with me, and she was a great comfort to me. She explained how it would be to see the baby since he had already passed, and her words brought me peace. After twelve hours of labor, my Zachary was born. My doctor gently explained that he had been dead longer than they had anticipated and that he had become "macerated." It was recommended that I not see him, and I was too weakened by medication to argue.

One of my nurses later returned to my room—I could see

my sorrow reflected in her eyes, and I was grateful for her kindness. She brought me a beautiful gift: a certificate with Zachary's footprints inked on it. I wanted to disappear into my bed.

My dear friends Laurel and Jim (Madison's godparents) had taken Madison to their house when this was happening. As I lay in my hospital bed on that third day of my ordeal, I heard Jim's and Laurel's voices and then a giggle from the hallway. There was Madison. She ran into the room and leapt on my bed. She hugged me so tight that she took my breath away, and my heart skipped as I realized how blessed I was to still have this precious, loving, beautiful child in my arms. She helped to ease my pain, but I still felt a sense of brokenness.

I stayed out of school for a week, and I was nervous to return. Everyone had known about my pregnancy—I had already been showing, and the kids had already started suggesting baby names. I tentatively walked into homeroom, willing myself to show a brave face for my kids. As I stood in front of the class, staring blankly in search of the right words, Nicole got up out of her chair, quietly walked up to me, and put her arms around me. Then Kristie followed suit. Then another child and another. I soon found myself in the midst of thirty hugs, enveloped by love. No words were spoken; none were needed. Their actions said it all. I was twenty-six years old, and I truly realized for the first time what it means to surround yourself with others who can fill your soul.

And so, I have been intentionally seeking out relationships with individuals who make me better than I am ever since. My journey to start RCA began with such a person in the fall of 2000.

The grandiose chandeliers and plush furnishings of the

Century Plaza Hotel in Los Angeles were beautiful yet imposing, as I stood mingling with some of the best educators in the country, nervously wringing my hands and trying to steady my quivering smile. We had gathered for the Disney American Teacher Awards, where I was one of thirty-three nominees. I was feeling awkward, overwhelmed, and unsure of myself. All of the other attendees seemed supremely confident and polished, and I couldn't stop myself from overanalyzing everything I said. I willed myself to believe that everyone else was as nervous as I was, but deep inside I felt much like an awkward seventh-grade girl who is trying to find a place to sit during lunch.

I was greatly relieved when an enthusiastic ten-year-old girl walked up to me, shook my hand, introduced herself, and said, "Hello! I am Rubina. It's so nice to meet you. I am really impressed that you hold a fashion show to teach descriptive writing. Can you tell me more about it?"

Wow, I thought. *Disney really, really knows how to pay attention to detail. This actress is great!*

I continued to be impressed as numerous children approached me, shook my hand, and continued to engage in the most sophisticated, yet genuine conversations. I was mesmerized. It occurred to me that these children were more at ease in this situation than I was, and my heart was deeply touched by the sparkle in their eyes and their obvious respect for one another. They radiated joy. Who on earth were these children, and where did they learn such poise?

Imagine my surprise when I learned that they weren't Disney ambassadors—they were the current students of the youngest of the honorees, a twenty-nine-year-old teacher from Harlem

BONDING

named Ron Clark. Ron approached me and shook my hand. After that moment, my life would never be the same.

There are times when we each encounter a small handful of people who we instantly know are destined for great things. These individuals possess a certain quality—some call it the *it* factor—that sets them apart. Quite simply, Ron had *it*. Call it charisma, call it drive, call it determination, but whatever you choose as a label, you know it when you see it. We became fast friends that week. We shared a sense of humor, and most important, we shared a passion for teaching. I was inspired by the brilliance, poise, charm, and confidence that he instilled in his students, and I wanted to have the same influence on mine. Over the years that followed, Ron became like a brother to me, as he taught me to have big dreams. And it was he who asked me to join him in cofounding the Ron Clark Academy, the school that would forever change my life.

I am often asked about the key to RCA's success. Well, for one thing, it is sheer hard work. But second, it is the team that we have assembled—I hire people I *admire*. I hire people who can help us grow professionally and personally because of the gifts that they possess. They are the people whom others love to be surrounded by—supremely talented and dynamic people, but also supremely *good* people. They are the type of people who make us all even better than we were before they entered our lives.

As parents and educators, we all tell our children to "choose your friends wisely." We love it when our children surround themselves with other kids who have good character, a strong work ethic, and a cheerful disposition. We tell students that they are often influenced by the friendships they keep, and we encourage them to seek out positive peer relationships. We harp on the relationships our children gravitate toward, and we don't hesitate to tell our children when they are hanging out with the wrong crowd. Yet as adults, we often fail to adhere to these guidelines. We all need to know when it is best to walk away.

My former school had a picturesque lake located behind it where teachers would often conduct their lessons. The lake was framed by a large athletic field that was maintained by a very masculine, muscle-bound, gun-shootin', huntin'-lovin', tobacco-chewin' groundskeeper named Dwayne.

One crisp spring morning, our science teacher, Mrs. Kurfess, took her sixth-grade class to the lake for a biology lesson. The students were having an absolutely lovely day as they quietly studied the marine life and recorded their findings in their journals. At the time, I was the school's principal, and I was en route to the gymnasium when shrill screaming, shrieking, and sobbing startled me. I took off as fast as my four-inch heels would carry me in the direction of the noise, and as I approached, I saw Mrs. Kurfess and twenty-five children huddled together with horrified expressions on their faces—they were all watching Dwayne.

Dwayne was gripping a four-foot-long snake by the tail. It flailed uncontrollably as he repeatedly beat it against a large boulder. Over and over again he pounded it. To be clear, the children weren't screaming because there was a snake. They were screaming because he was violently hurting it. "Please stop! Don't! You're killing it!" was the continuous refrain, but Dwayne's eyes bulged wildly as he gripped harder and swung faster. I was dumbfounded.

Mrs. Kurfess yelled, "You're scaring the children!" But

Dwayne swung and swung like Paul Bunyan chopping trees until the snake went limp. Finally, he dropped it at his feet, wiped his brow, looked at me, and said, "Phew—that could have hurt one of the kids!"

Honestly, from there the story is somewhat of a blur—I know that I took twenty-five crying children inside and started to work on damage control before fifty angry parents and PETA showed up at my office door.

There are some deadly "snakes" out there. However, we don't have to beat them over the head to get on with our lives. Sometimes we need to remain calm, continue on our path, and learn to peacefully coexist with them. Sometimes we just need to leave them alone.

When you are with your friends, do you feel better or worse after you leave them? If you feel worse, then why on earth are you devoting precious time to those relationships? We tell our kids to do this—be nice, get along, and ignore others when they aren't acting the way that they should. But as adults, we often find it harder to do. If your close friendships are not healthy, then you need to cultivate new relationships. If the problem lies with your coworkers, it can become trickier. You must obviously interact with them in a professional and kind way—remember, you set the tone. You cannot ignore them, but I once heard a wise preacher say, "If you are walking away from something, then you are walking toward something else."

Walk toward individuals who exude excellence and goodness, and surround yourself with those who make you a better person. Bond with individuals who are good for your soul.

CLASS NOTES

- Surround yourself with others who will fill your soul.
- Seek out relationships with individuals whom you admire and who will make you a better person.
- Be kind to everyone—don't judge. However, spend less time on unhealthy relationships, and walk away from those who are harmful to your growth.

HOMEWORK

1. Consider whom you spend most of your time with. Are the relationships healthy ones? If not, evaluate why and determine if there is a way that you can turn them around. Be honest with yourself. Do you need to walk away from some relationships?
2. Make a list of the people in your circle whom you admire the most. What qualities make you feel this way? Is there a way that you can spend more time with these individuals? How can you also cultivate more of these relationships?

14

CREATIVITY

———— COURSE DESCRIPTION ————
In this course, you will learn how to nurture the ingenuity
and originality of others.

There was no doubt that Dustin was bright. He made good grades in every class, and he was known for acing almost every test in every class with little to no studying. He was a handsome, friendly kid who had dimples and a perpetual smirk on his face, like he was privy to a private joke that no one else knew. School was a breeze for him, and he approached it as nonchalantly as a day at the beach. Dustin was certainly a smart kid, but he was bored to death. So when he entered my class fifteen years ago, I was determined to change this.

Truth be told, I knew that Dustin would probably continue to make good grades, go to a good college, and have a solid career one day. But I wanted Dustin to know the joy of learning—to have a fire and a drive that pushed him to unlock every bit of greatness within him. I didn't want him to settle. And while I place a huge emphasis on academic rigor, I knew that I still hadn't found the key to Dustin's potential—until we had our big fashion extravaganza.

On the day of our descriptive writing fashion show, the workers for each clothing line quickly readied their models for the catwalk. Nick put on his work boots, plaid jacket, striped shirt, red felt sash, fur-lined cap, and sunglasses; a blue sequined skirt, striped socks, a black cape, purple wig, and white sun hat completed Jackie's ensemble. Such attire was typical for the Fashion Extravaganza, for the students' task was to create a hideous, mismatched line of clothing. The catch: they had to market and write about this clothing line in such a magnificent way that surely everyone would want to buy it.

The lights were dimmed, the spotlight set, the microphones checked, and the pulsating music cued. As each model strutted down the catwalk lit up with tube lights, another student read the detailed description about the model's spectacular ensemble.

And then Dustin stepped to the mic. He smiled, but it wasn't his usual bemused grin. There was an intensity that I hadn't seen before. He cleared his throat and began. "Today, Jeff is sporting the hottest trend for fall: the cardboard box hat! Versatile and fully recyclable, this hat can go from day to night with a simple lid change. Also note the clean, sleek lines of his arm guards; lightweight and functional, they provide protection from even the bleakest of weather. Available in a variety of colors, every one of today's ensembles has been painstakingly handcrafted from fine quality cardboard and duct tape, imported from China. They are a must-have for every man on the go. . . ."

As his teammates dramatically strutted and posed, all of our mouths fell open. Apparently, Dustin had spent hours making every one of their ensembles by hand, using only duct tape and cardboard. And while they were obviously absurd, they were also beautifully and brilliantly created. I had never seen anything like it. We all stood and burst into roaring applause when the last member of his group left the catwalk. And as Dustin took a bow, I saw the look on his face—he knew that he had accomplished something. He had shown us all the creativity that was within him. Every detail in those costumes and every word of his speech was perfect.

As you might imagine, Dustin got major props from his classmates that day. As the year went on, he became known as the most creative kid in class, and he embraced the title wholeheartedly. He pushed himself to come up with the most unusual and unique ideas; he became the "go-to" guy when others wanted to find a way to look at something differently.

In education, the phrase "think outside the box" has been used far too often; we have become immune to the term. But it is also true that far too often, we try to fit kids into a one-size-fits-all mold, and in doing so, we prevent them from showing the world their unlimited potential. Think about it this way: if you keep shoving things into a box, eventually the box breaks. And that is what we are doing to many of society's most innovative minds.

Now, Dustin was a happy, well-adjusted kid, but sometimes the most creative kids are the loners—the shy, awkward, or quirky ones who just don't know how to fit in very well. Yes, creative kids have to learn how to adjust to society's rules and structure, but we also have to find ways to give them an outlet for their creativity. And actually, we need to do even more than that—we have to embrace their unique ideas and nurture them.

Stevie was one of the loners. When he entered my sixth-grade class, I had already been given the heads-up about his sullen demeanor, his extreme introversion, and his reluctance to engage and interact with others. Stevie was the kid who would rather work alone, sit by himself, and read. That year, I required my students to compose a narrative as their first major writing assignment, and on the day it was due, I thought that it would be a great idea to share our stories and celebrate them in a unique way.

I borrowed some tents, sleeping bags, and camping equipment, and set up Camp Sharastorie in my room. I downloaded nature sound effects and made a campfire by surrounding a fake Halloween cauldron (the kind with a fan, cloth flames, and a red light) with firewood. After buying some marshmallows and scrounging up some flashlights, I was ready to go. It was the first of my "magical transformations" of that school year, so I couldn't wait to see the expressions on my new students' faces.

They were excited, no doubt. As we huddled around the campfire and began to read our narratives aloud, I was surprised when Stevie was among the first to volunteer. He grabbed a flashlight and began to read with such animation and emotion that it put the other classmates' attempts to shame. For almost ten minutes he shared his tale of an epic battle in another world. And we were mesmerized. Stevie had come out of his box.

After that day, Stevie was still quirky and socially awkward, but he had an outlet for his creativity, and he began to flourish. The kids told him that they wanted to hear more of the story, so he wrote pages and pages that he would bring to lunch each day. Huddled around him at the lunch table, a group of little boys became Stevie's friends as he transported them to the fantastical world that he had created in his limitless imagination.

So what about you? Are you stuck in a box? Time and time again, I have heard adults comment that they do not believe that they are creative. If this applies to you, practice trying to think more creatively, and you will be surprised with the results.

As a young girl, I was the type of student who wanted everything to be precise and correct—I hated open-ended assignments because I wasn't sure I'd have the "right" answer. I was a good student, but I do not have a single recollection of anyone ever referring to me as a creative thinker.

It was not until I was three or four years into my teaching career that I began to evolve. I was actually inspired by my daughter and my students—I had such admiration for those who thought in new or different ways; I wanted to be more like them and to encourage others to see the value of their talents as well. I set off on a quest to be creative—and yes, I did it methodically, like any precise, Type A personality would do. An amazing thing happened: it worked.

Some of my most creative teaching ideas I credit to my relationship with my former co-teacher, Amy Loiselle. Anytime I had a new or different idea, Amy was the first to say, "Ooo! Yes! And let's also do this!" Together, we dreamed of lessons filled with magic and innovation. From turning our classroom into *Survivor* base camp to creating the mountains of Utah during the Winter Olympics, Amy sparked my creativity in ways that no one else had before. Perhaps our first co-creation came about when we were teaching punctuation to our students, and we needed a way to make it more hands-on. I think I had mentioned using pasta as a manipulative, and before I knew it, Amy was making placemats with sentences that needed commas, quotation marks, semicolons, and capitalization. Punctuatiano's was opened for business, and hundreds of students have dined there ever since. In fact, my current students recently dined there for the first time.

"Welcome to Punctuatiano's! My name is Isabella, and I will be your host and server. How many are dining with you?" I asked.

"Mrs. Bearden, um, I mean Miss Isabella, we have a party of four," Regan giggled.

"Excellent, follow me! Will the rest of you please hold on a moment until I can seat you? We have a short wait today."

As the students entered my classroom, they discovered that the typical desks were gone. Instead, they were seated at tables covered with plastic red-checkered tablecloths, vases with red carnations, and battery-operated candles that flickered in the dimmed room. "O Sole Mio" played over the speakers as I, dressed in my tuxedo shirt, bow tie, and cummerbund, escorted each dinner party to their reserved tables.

"Thank you for dining at Punctuatiano's, where we punctuate with pasta! Tonight our specials include comma calzones, semicolon spaghetti, and quotations with Alfredo sauce. I'd like to direct your attention to the *whine* list . . . note I said 'whine list.' It contains all the things that you all are always whining about."

Matthew said, "Miss, I would like a bottle of 'I have so much studying to do' when you have get the chance."

Maleigha added, "Ooo, yea! I have drunk a lot of that!"

As students burst out laughing, I tried my best to keep in character.

After explaining the rules, I served the students paper dishes full of sentences that weren't punctuated, and the students used uncooked elbow macaroni, spaghetti, and pastina to make their corrections. They were served several courses, each more "academically filling" than the last.

"Miss Isabella," said Kalani, "please give my compliments to the chef. I found today's main course to be especially filling!"

Terrell nodded. "Yes, Miss Bearden—I mean Miss Isabella. I am getting kind of full. Can I just have the rest in a doggie bag?"

As their jokes continued, so did the learning. As it was time to leave, I received great "tips."

"Thank you for the lesson," said Lizzie. "I never knew that punctuation could be so fun!"

"Can we do this again tomorrow?" asked Ashton.

Daryl Ann said, "Thank you, Mrs. Bearden . . . uh, I mean Isabella, for doing this for us. I love punctuating now."

"Me, too!" said Mariah and D'Nai.

Natalie added, "Mrs. Bearden, I love how you always make us look at things in a different way. It makes the world seem so much more . . . creative."

I encourage everyone to seek out ways to express themselves more creatively. It might be through music, it might be through art. Perhaps you should start that blog or find ways to open that business. Make cakes, learn a new language, take up photography, write poetry, go to dance class. Just do something—anything—to keep the lid off your creativity. Your options are limitless—isn't that exciting?

CREATIVITY

CLASS NOTES

- We often stifle the creativity of others by forcing them to fit into the boxes that we create.
- When we continue to force others to conform, sometimes it breaks their creative spirit.
- Some people who are bored are really in need of a creative outlet.
- Some of the most withdrawn or introverted individuals can also be the most creative.
- We can all increase our capacity for creative thought.

HOMEWORK

1. Think about the children whom you teach or influence. Do you encourage or stifle their creativity? Look for ways to help them express themselves.
2. Seek opportunities to bask in others' creativity. Go to more museums, attend more shows or concerts, read more books, spend more time with creative people—commit to finding influences that will spark your inner creative abilities.
3. Sign up for that class or those lessons today. What are you waiting for?

15

IMPROVISATION

===== COURSE DESCRIPTION =====
In this course, you will learn how to get positive results when things
don't go as planned.

"Down, set, hike!" I blew my referee whistle, and the Grammar
Bowl began.

The desks and chairs had been cleared out, and yard lines
marked the football field that spanned the length of my classroom. It was Red versus Blue, and the stakes were high: the
winning team would be deemed the Grammar Bowl Champions.

As the students answered questions on their ActivExpres-
sions, our electronic student response systems, they maneuvered down the field to the end zone. If a correct answer was
given, the student was told, "Roll for yardage!" He would then

roll a die to determine how many yards had been earned. If an incorrect answer was given, the student received a "Fumble!" and had to remain in the same place.

Dressed in my referee uniform, I ran up and down the field to enforce the rules. Students who received a penalty flag for any reason, such as off-task behavior, were given a fifteen-yard penalty. As students proceeded up and down the field to "Glory, Glory to Old Georgia," they celebrated touchdowns and continued play.

At the end of each quarter, the players became the band as we reviewed with music. As the song "Low" came over the speakers, we sang our own version of the lyrics:

They modify adverbs, adjectives, and verbs
Some end in -ly, they're describing words
They tell us more, that is for sure;
Adverbs we know know know know know know know
*They also answer **Where? How? How much? When?***
***To what extent?** Please listen up my friend.*
*They tell us **Why?** Isn't that fly?*
Adverbs we know know know know know know know

Throughout the game, we practiced punctuation marks using referee hand signals—a touchdown signal was used for quotations, clipping became a question mark. We all moved with precision, punctuating even the most difficult of sentences.

The Grammar Bowl was high-energy, rigorous, and tremendous fun. When the final buzzer rang on the scoreboard, it was time to reflect on the learning process.

"What did you find to be the most difficult challenge for you?" I asked.

Divine responded, "When I became stuck on certain sentences, I was so frustrated to see other students quickly gaining more yardage."

"So what did you do?"

"I changed my strategy. I realized that I was repeatedly making the same mistakes, so I had to stop and ask myself the right questions in order to answer correctly," she said.

"Bingo!" I said. "Why were you missing some of the questions?" I asked the class.

D'Nai answered, "I was rushing to try to finish first. When I stopped and thought about what I knew, I was able to answer better."

"Same with me," added Tessema. "I was excited to try to get a touchdown, so I made careless mistakes."

"True," I said. "And what if we aren't rushing but we still make mistakes?"

"Well, in that case," said Mariah, "we do the best we can to figure out why we are making the mistakes and try to solve the problem."

Ogechi added, "Yeah, and sometimes it helps to sing a little."

Good point, Ogechi. Good point.

In many of life's situations, there are detours and roadblocks that keep us from reaching our desired destination. When we encounter them, we have two choices: we can continue driving forward, or we can give up. But first, we have to accept that things don't always go as planned; we have to be willing to recalculate our route.

I am always looking for new ideas for my classroom, so when I heard that some teachers were using exercise balls for student seats, I couldn't wait to get a set of my own. Upon further research, I read claims that sitting on the balls could improve posture, strengthen core muscles, and even help restless learners concentrate better. I simply had to try them, so I obtained the funding and purchased my own set.

On the day that they arrived, our counselor Ms. Scott helped me inflate them, and I set the blue orbs all around my room and stacked the chairs in the back. Each ball had a base to help with stability, and I had even ordered different sizes for different-sized students. I followed all of the guidelines that teachers had suggested.

The students entered my classroom, smiling in surprise, and eagerly took a seat. I thoroughly explained the rules for sitting correctly and for the care of the balls, and then I began my lesson on dangling participles. At RCA, we have strict guidelines for students in our classes, and they are supposed to track the teacher when she is talking, sit up straight, and focus. Well, all of those learned behaviors were quickly thrown out the window. I looked out to find a sea of swaying, bobbing, and bouncing children—their movement made me queasy.

Again I explained my expectations, but despite their best efforts, it was impossible for the kids to balance on those balls without swirling and bouncing. Undaunted, I continued with my lesson.

"Where is the participial phrase in this sentence, Justyn?" I asked.

"Well, the phrase is . . ." *Thud.* Justyn rolled off the ball and fell onto the floor. We couldn't help but laugh once we realized that he was okay.

"Leanetta, why is the phrase written incorrectly?" I continued.

"Well, the . . . participial . . . phrase . . . modifies . . . the . . . wrong . . . noun . . . and . . . it . . . is . . . confusing. . . ." Leanetta bounced in between every word as she gave her answer.

"Jordan, why didn't you clap with the rest of the class when Leanetta gave her answer?" I reprimanded.

"Mrs. Bearden, I'm sorry, but if I let go of my desk, I will fall over!" he exclaimed.

It was a mess. If I didn't know better, I would have thought that mischievous ghosts were circling above the class with huge mallets, playing one heck of a game of Whack-A-Mole. I am a firm believer in the need for movement in the classroom—I use music, dance, games, and all types of techniques to keep kids active, but I couldn't stand the constant jiggling while I was talking. It made me nutty.

Days two and three were no better. For the next few days, I tried to think of possible solutions. Finally, I decided to allow students to use their old chairs if they preferred them. More than half of them opted for the chairs at first, and by the end of the week, the balls were deflated and packed away.

I was deflated, too. The balls had worked in other classrooms, so surely I could have made them work in mine. I shared my frustrations with the class.

A'Lyric laughed, "It's okay, Mrs. Bearden. They just didn't work for us. Maybe we have less balance!"

Jordan added, "I thought that they were fun, but they actually made it harder for me to concentrate. I was too busy thinking about how I was sitting to be able to focus on anything else!"

"But for some reason, they have worked beautifully in other classrooms!" I argued.

Jule said, "But Mrs. Bearden, we aren't other classrooms—we are our own class. We aren't like anyone else. It is okay if it didn't work for us. We have plenty of other things that we do that no other class in the world does."

"Yes," added Dasia. "At least you tried!"

And so my students put it all into perspective for me. I will always continue to try new things, but I must remind myself that what works for someone else might not work for me, and what works for one group of students just might not work for another. I have since seen some amazing classrooms where exercise balls are utilized beautifully, but I accept that they just aren't for me to use in my class. And that is okay.

I was willing to take a detour. In fact, sometimes detours lead us to the greatest adventures of all.

When we took our fifth graders to New York City, our time was spent visiting museums and embracing the city's rich culture and history, in addition to participating in our own Amazing Race. Our schedule was packed, but while there, we discovered that President Obama was making a special visit to Ground Zero to lay a wreath in memory of the victims of 9/11.

The city was abuzz with talk of the president's arrival, and the news stations anticipated that thousands would line the streets near Ground Zero in hopes of getting a glimpse of him. This all became a huge dilemma for us. Should we go ahead with our agenda, or should we join the multitudes of others who were going to crowd the sidewalks? This was our one opportunity to see the city, but on the other hand, this might also be our one opportunity to see the president of the United States. We weren't sure what to do, so we asked the kids what they preferred.

Hands down, they chose to go to Ground Zero. We made it clear that it was highly unlikely that we would see President Obama, but they were willing to take the gamble. So, we maneuvered thirty fifth-grade students from subway to street after street, and as we approached our destination, the journey became more and more impossible.

Throngs of people lined the streets and pushed up against the metal railings that were used to block the crowds from overflowing into the roads. Our chaperones were somewhat nervous—corralling thirty kids in such crowds was no easy feat. We became increasingly frustrated, too, as we realized that the distance to the street was ten to fifteen people thick, and no one was budging. We turned right, we turned left, and time and time again we hit roadblocks formed by people or the police.

Somehow we were being led farther and farther away from our destination; the path we were being forced to take was not the one we had chosen. Things were not going as planned, and I feared that the whole experience would be a colossal waste of time.

As we walked down a less crowded street, farther from Ground Zero, we were contemplating returning to the subway when I noticed a bank of news cameras. They were all lining one particular corner, and my radar went up. Immediately, we tried to maneuver the kids to a spot on the same road as they, but others were smart enough to catch on, too. I went to one of the photographers and said, "Excuse me, but is the president expected to come this way?"

"We don't know. There have been several alternate routes given, so no one is sure. However, this seems the most likely route to us."

I thanked him, just as the police politely told us we had to move; we were in the middle of the street, and we had to get back on the sidewalks—sidewalks that were now completely impassable. I sighed, and we turned to go down a small, empty, one-way street. We walked by several police officers and smiled and nodded. We felt defeated, and we pulled out our maps to find the nearest subway. Chandler ran up to me and said, "Mrs. Bearden, that police officer said that he is going to come this way."

"What? Really? He told you that?"

"No, ma'am, but when we were walking by, I heard one police officer tell the other, 'He is coming this way.'"

"Honey, you must be mistaken; this is a one-way street, and it would take the president in the opposite direction. Are you sure?"

"Yes, ma'am. That's what I heard him say."

So I walked up to the police officer and asked, "Sir, excuse me. Is it possible that President Obama will be coming down this street?"

He smiled. "Well, even if he were, I wouldn't be able to tell you." And he winked. At least I thought he winked. *Did he wink or did I imagine it?*

"Kids, stand along these barricades—quick!" I instructed as

we formed a line along the small side street—thirty-six of us all in the front row—and waited. And waited. We were the only ones there. It was cold, and the longer we waited, the more my doubts grew. We learned that the president had already gone to the site but I thought there was still hope that we could see him on his way to the airport. I looked down the row of my precious students, so wide-eyed, anxious, and patient, and I hoped that they wouldn't be heartbroken.

And then, things quickly started to happen. Three Secret Service men walked down the street, looking ominously to and fro. They spoke into earpieces, and a group of five more appeared as if out of thin air. They looked up at the high-rise buildings around us and started to yell at people to close the windows. When those who were in the windows didn't comply immediately, the Secret Service yelled more forcefully.

People started to file from the other side streets onto ours when they noticed the commotion, but they had to stand behind us. Suddenly, a horde of police motorcycles, SUVs, and limousines proceeded down the street en masse, going the wrong way. Sneaky plan! We stood, mesmerized, as the motorcade passed us, each vehicle looking more important than the last. And then President Obama's limousine drove past— he looked out his window and waved to us as my students bounced and bobbed and waved in sheer delight. No matter what your political viewpoints are, you must realize how thrilling this was for my students, thus making it pure joy for me. It was a beautiful moment.

If we had been able to stop at any other place along our route, we would not have been as close to the president or have been able to see him. Yet, time and time again we were led on a different path than the one that we had intended, and when we took time to watch and listen, we noticed the signs. By allowing ourselves to be aware of the messages, we learned that a better path was intended for us, and we experienced one of those once-in-a-lifetime moments as a result.

We are sometimes hit with obstacle after obstacle, and we allow these to defeat us or we give up. Obstacles are not there to make us quit; rather, they are there to direct us to take another route—one that we would not have chosen otherwise. We miss the meaning, though, if we don't notice the signs along the way. Every single life has twists and turns, setbacks and detours. The roadblocks are a part of our unique journey— we must accept that the mystery ahead is what allows us to live with the thrill of anticipation. We all have different life maps, and each continues to unfold with all its beauty, pain, wonder, and drama. After all, our problems do not define us; how we respond to them does.

If we can instill this spirit of resilience in our children, then they will be able to handle life's problems with greater ease— even with a greater sense of humor. After all, when the going gets tough, the tough start laughing.

Last autumn my students and I had the opportunity to visit a farm set deep in the country, and we thought that we had died and landed in heaven. We were surrounded everywhere by rolling hills, meadows, and trees exploding with autumn hues. As we walked down the long path to the cabin, the sun was beginning to set, and I told Ron that we simply had to get some pictures in the meadow before it grew too dark.

IMPROVISATION

I quickly grabbed several students who were playing ball in the adjacent field and asked them if they would like to join us for our impromptu photo shoot. Tessema and Natalie readily joined us, and then Regan, Chandler, Daryl Ann, Matthew, Trinity, and Kalani soon followed. Off we set off across the vast meadow. The October air was crisp and clean, the breeze was gentle, and the grass formed a soft carpet beneath us as we approached a tree in the distance.

So there we were, living out our very own picture postcard moment. And then . . . Kalani started to sink into the ground. And then Tessema. And Trinity. And then everyone else. Seems that we had strolled across that beautiful meadow . . . only to find ourselves sinking deeply into manure.

"Oh, noooo . . . Mrs. Bearden! Help!" exclaimed Tessema as the muck completely enveloped his feet.

Daryl Ann shrieked, "I'm sinking. I'm completely stuck. Help! What do I do?"

Natalie hollered, "Yuck! My shoes are completely covered, and I can feel it seeping into my socks and in between my toes!"

This stuff was like quicksand. The more we tried to avoid it, the deeper we sank. And somehow, we couldn't find a viable, manure-free escape route.

"I think it is worse if we stay still!" I exclaimed. "Let's try to run. Grab someone's hand so you don't fall, and go as quickly as you can!" I said while struggling not to tumble over myself.

Trinity laughed as she looked at my feet and noted, "Mrs. Bearden, only you would run through manure in four-inch heels!"

As we all started to sink ever deeper, there was only one thing we could do: laugh. Hard. Deep belly laughs that somehow rendered us even less coordinated and unable to free ourselves. The absurdity of it was not lost on any of us, and so we giggled as we worked to free our feet from the horrid, smelly ooze. Those who escaped first grabbed the hands of the others to help them across, and we jumped, dodged, and hopped our way out of that meadow, covered with a slimy dark mess. After futile attempts to hose ourselves off, we collapsed in the cabin, retelling our tale and reliving the laughter all over again.

Sometimes in life, you find yourself surrounded by all kinds of crap. But my students reminded me that when that happens, accept it, put on some fabulous heels, laugh, grab hold of someone's hand, and skip on through it.

IMPROVISATION

- When things go awry, we must have resilience.
- Sometimes the solution is different than we imagined.
- We don't always get what we want in life. The detours are often exactly what we needed instead.
- Our problems don't define us; how we respond to them does.
- When life gets difficult, look for reasons to laugh.

HOMEWORK

1. The next time you are faced with a problem, do not let it paralyze you. Instead, brainstorm possible solutions. Seek guidance from others if you need to.
2. When things don't work out as you intended, actively look for the positive things that could result from the situation. Find ways to focus on possible ways to turn the negatives into positives.
3. If things are especially difficult, surround yourself with people and things that make you laugh. Watch a comedy; read a funny book; choose to do something lighthearted so that you do not wallow in pity.

16

GRATITUDE

═══════════ COURSE DESCRIPTION ═══════════
In this course, you will learn how to cherish the things
that truly matter.

Jevon was a tough kid. Throughout his childhood, he had learned to develop barriers from people as a form of survival, and bouts of anger were well documented in his school records when we admitted him as a fifth-grade student. However, my staff and I look below the surface of our students, and underneath Jevon's harsh exterior, we saw resiliency, brilliance, and a heart that loved fiercely and loyally.

Jevon's fifth-grade year was marked with numerous detentions for frequently talking out of turn, interrupting others, and failing to complete work. But with consistent love, patience, discipline, and support from all of us, he has grown into one of the finest young men one could imagine. The transformation was not a quick one, but as we balanced our discipline with love, the detentions and misbehavior became less and less frequent, and the respect from his peers grew as his leadership capabilities became evident. Our whole staff spent a lot of extra time with Jevon, attending his games, working with him on assignments, and mentoring him. So when Jevon entered the eighth grade and his family found themselves without anywhere to live, Ron and I knew that we needed to do all that we could to help.

Jevon's grandmother worked two jobs to support her grandchildren, but despite her best efforts, life had continued to knock her down. So much so that the family was forced to move to get away from an unhealthy situation. She was appreciative when we found her an affordable house to rent. But it took prodding on our part to discover that although the family would now have a roof over their heads, the house would be devoid of furniture and in much need of repairs.

Ron and I realized that there was more we could do, so we sent emails to several friends, and the response was overwhelming. Together, we compiled furniture and other household items. People volunteered to help with painting and minor repairs. However, since Jevon's grandmother was one who never wanted to impose, we knew that this would need to be done as a surprise. After a little craftiness on our part, Ron and I got the key to the house two days before the family was to relocate.

Our friends and staff members brought over sofas, pictures, dishes, towels, and bedding. One family even bought brand-new bedroom furniture and a kitchen table. As the house began to take shape, our hearts filled; we knew that the family would be thrilled. We spent hours decorating each room with plants, flowers, and pictures of family members in beautiful frames; we even stocked the refrigerator and pantry. Jevon's sister's room was decorated with beautiful colors, toys, art, and little feminine touches that we knew she would love. Special effort was put into making Jevon's room reflect his bold personality, too; we filled it with bright colors and pictures of special moments at RCA.

Two days later, I met Jevon and his grandmother to return the key. I had intended to hand it to them and leave before they went inside, but they asked if I would like to stay a minute. When we walked into the house, Jevon's grandmother gasped, covering her mouth. Then tears streamed down her cheeks. She was speechless as she stood looking at her new living room and kitchen.

"It is all yours," I said.

She could only continue to hold her hand over her mouth and shake her head crying.

"There's more," I said. "Would you like to see it?"

"More?" she whispered. "This is already so much . . . too much."

As we walked down the hallway, I told Jevon where his room was, expecting him to want to see it right away. Instead, he followed his grandmother and me into his little sister's bedroom. It was there that he took delight—not in what would be in his room, but in his baby sister's room. His happiness for her was so very evident as he started crying. Nothing else mattered.

Jevon did love his room, too, but it was the way that he reveled in his sister's blessing that affected me the most that morning. Here was a child who had very little, but who was filled with gratitude when he knew that his sister would have a bedroom like other little girls. His selfless appreciation overwhelmed me. In that moment, I made a silent vow to never take any blessing for granted.

Appreciation is an art that takes commitment and, at times, practice. We often get so busy thinking about what we do not have and what we cannot do that we fail to capture life's beauty. But if we commit to taking the time to stop and give thanks, we see that our world is full of abundant blessings at every turn. Belinda, a student whom I taught sixteen years ago, helped me understand this.

Every teacher can appreciate a mature, sensible, and eager student like Belinda. She was in my seventh-grade class at a school where I taught in an affluent Atlanta suburb. She didn't live in the same school zone, but she was allowed to attend since her grandmother drove a school bus for the district. She would rise at 5 A.M. each day and ride her grandmother's entire route before arriving at school, which made it all the more incredible that she would always stop by to help organize my room before her morning classes began.

Although Belinda's family didn't have the affluence of others, she carried herself with a self-assuredness that I admired. A tomboy who didn't wear the same high-end-brand clothing as her peers, she preferred blue jeans and her navy windbreaker and was set apart from the other middle school girls. But all the students respected her and often looked to her for leadership, advice, and mediation for middle school girl drama. She was admired like a big sister, even though she was no older than her classmates.

Late one afternoon, I saw Belinda waiting in front of the school for a ride. When I asked her why no one had picked her up yet, she explained that she needed to make up a test, and her grandfather was having car trouble. She would have to wait until her grandmother finished all of her routes before she could phone her to get a ride home. I offered to take her myself. She hesitated a moment, smiled, and called her grandfather so that we could ask him if it would be okay.

When we got into the car, Belinda thanked me profusely and asked if I was sure I wanted to do this since she lived so far away. I told her it wasn't a problem and that I wanted to catch up on how she was doing. The conversation was so enjoyable that the drive through Atlanta rush hour and meandering backstreets didn't seem nearly as long as it was. When I thanked Belinda for always being a voice of reason among her peers, she smiled and said, "Well, some of these girls just haven't figured out what really matters yet. They are more concerned with what others think of them than how they treat people. It's like . . . they base who they are on what they have and what they want others to see. It's kinda sad if you think about it."

After our forty-five-minute drive, we arrived at Belinda's home. What I saw broke my heart. The dirt yard was littered with broken bikes, a Big Wheel, and a few scattered potted plants that had been abandoned long ago. The cracked sidewalk led to a small gray box with two windows, peeling paint, and a torn screen door set atop three broken, crooked steps.

Belinda looked at the house, smiled at me, and said, "Well, this is it. It is pretty bad, isn't it?"

I didn't know how to answer that question, so I asked one of my own. "Who lives here with you?"

"My grandparents, my big sister, and my little brother. It is all we can afford since my grandfather is on disability. It is okay, though—we are happy here."

I swallowed hard and asked, "Do you all need anything?"

She replied, "No, ma'am. We are good. This is just a house. One day, I will buy a nicer one for my whole family."

"Belinda, I think that you will be able to accomplish anything you set your mind to do—you are really special."

"Yes, ma'am," she said grinning. "Don't worry about me. Things aren't that important to me. I know exactly who I am."

As she thanked me and walked away, I realized how beautiful it was that this precious thirteen-year-old child knew more about what matters in life than most adults. Belinda was surrounded each day by very wealthy children who had the best that money could buy, yet she remained unfazed by it all. She was content to be who she was and to have the things that were important: a close-knit family, an education, the friendship and respect of her peers, her health, a brilliant mind, and a bright future.

There is nothing wrong with having nice things, but we sometimes misplace our focus in the pursuit of them and feel empty, despite the fact that we continue to have more possessions than ever before. Look, I have an unhealthy obsession with shoes, and I love a great purse as much as the next girl. But when I find myself thinking that I *need* these things instead of the fact that I just *want* them, I often reflect on the lessons children have taught me that relationships matter a whole lot more than any material things ever will.

At RCA, we work to build a sense of community, and we believe in fostering relationships with every family. One of the ways that we do this is by visiting the homes of every new student before the first day of school. We want to show our families that we are a team, and that as a staff, we are willing to go above and beyond for our students. It is always a warm, happy experience. Well, almost always.

During one such home visit, Ron and I spent fifteen minutes driving up and down the aisles of a complex looking for Isaiah's apartment. The numbers marking the separate buildings had long since faded or fallen off the peeling wood. We tried to call Isaiah's mom's number, only to learn that the service had been cut off. After finding one clearly marked building, we counted our way to the one that we thought must be Isaiah's, walked to the door, and knocked. He stuttered a hello and invited us in.

Isaiah politely escorted us to a small love seat, and then he grabbed a wooden chair from the dining area so that he could join us. He just sat there staring at us until Ron asked, "Isaiah, where is your mom? Isn't she joining us?"

"Um . . . she had to work and couldn't get off to meet you. I didn't have a way to call you. I-I'm sorry."

"It's okay," I said. "But are you here alone?"

"No, um, my big brother is in his room."

"Can we meet him then?" I asked. I thought that I had heard some rustling coming from down the hall.

Isaiah hesitated, "Uh, sure . . . maybe when he wakes up." He quickly changed the subject. "I made you some cookies. Would you like one?"

"We'd love one!" Ron exclaimed.

As Isaiah walked into the kitchen, we took a few moments to survey the room. It was immaculate and barren. A single cross hung over the burgundy velour love seat. A small wooden table with a doily and a lamp sat in the other corner. Pink plastic flowers topped the old Formica table that filled the cramped dining area. Although there was little there, it was obvious that great care had been given to make the space as nice as possible. There was no coffee table, so we awkwardly adjusted our water and cookies in our laps as Isaiah stiffly sat back down in his wooden chair.

"So, buddy, we are just here to tell you how excited we are that you will be our student this year. You are going to have—" Ron stopped midsentence as an enormous tear spilled from Isaiah's eye and slowly ran down his cheek.

"Oh, sweetheart, what's wrong?" I asked.

It took him a moment to respond. "I am afraid that you don't like my house," he whispered, hanging his head.

A golf-ball-sized lump filled my throat as Ron and I simultaneously blurted, "Yes, we do!"

Ron commented on how comfortable the love seat was as I complimented the pink flowers. We told Isaiah how we weren't there to judge his house; we were there to show him how excited we were to have him as a student. He slowly started to relax and by the time we left, he was smiling slightly.

Over the next year, Isaiah proved to be one of the most

hardworking, extraordinary students at RCA. He was dedicated, kindhearted, and brilliant. Quick to show appreciation for even the smallest kindnesses, he was greatly loved by staff and students alike. And as we encouraged and validated him, his confidence continued to blossom. We spent time with his mother, too—she shared her son's work ethic and was doing all that she could to provide a good life for him.

Isaiah was thrilled when his mother married a kind man who seemed to embrace the role of stepfather. He smiled more, he talked about his family more, and it was obvious that a void in his life had been filled. The last week of school, Isaiah asked me when we would be doing our next home visit.

"Sweetie, we usually only do the summer visits for the new students."

"Oh," he said. "I was hoping you'd come to my house again."

"You know what? We'd be thrilled to come to your house again. We will be there!" I said.

So that August, we returned to Isaiah's apartment. This time he opened the door before we could knock. His smile was so big that his dimples showed as he led us into the living room. But this time, his mother stood in the kitchen making us a full meal, and his new stepfather entered to shake our hands and thank us for coming. His big brother came out to say hello, and Ron and I returned to our seats on the burgundy velour love seat. Another two chairs had been added, and pictures of the family had been set on the countertop. The apartment was pretty much the same—simple and immaculate—but it was no longer barren. It was now full of love, laughter, and happiness. Isaiah beamed throughout the visit, and as he walked us to our car, we told him how much we had enjoyed ourselves.

"I am so happy you came to see my house—I couldn't wait for you to see how nice it is now."

In Isaiah's eyes, his home was completely different. It was now filled with two extra chairs, some pictures . . . and a happy family.

I had mistaken Isaiah's embarrassment for a lack of material things. It wasn't until this second visit that I realized that it was the continuous absence of his mom and the withdrawal of his brother that had caused him sadness; it was a happy, unified family that he longed for. Isaiah could have lived in a mansion when we visited for the first time, and that emptiness still would have permeated the space. It was the relationships that mattered and gave him the fulfillment that he so desperately sought.

There is a certain energy, joy, and peace that individuals exude when they have an understanding of what truly matters in life. The children of South Africa imprinted this upon my heart when I first visited them in the spring of 2010.

Soweto is a township located near Johannesburg, South Africa. It was there that my students and I saw extreme poverty and precious, beautiful children who had so little but who loved so much. My students collected supplies for numerous schools; we delivered paper, pens, pencils, and more to students throughout Soweto. I was struck by the resilience of the people; their world was filled with song, despite the continuing plagues of poverty, racism, and lack of funding for their schools. Students were crammed into small, run-down classrooms, yet their eyes said, "Teach me!" Their faces lit up when we arrived, and everywhere we went, they laughed, clapped, sang for us, and thanked us profusely. The supplies were greatly needed; in fact, I opened a science textbook when visiting an overcrowded classroom with peeling plaster, chipped chalkboards, and shoddy wooden desks. The copyright date: 1956. However, more than anything, these children longed for hugs, for pictures, for simple interaction with my students. They were overjoyed to just visit and spend time with us.

After a long day of visiting several schools, we were completely drained, both physically and emotionally. Our local guide, Arthur, instructed our tour bus to pull up to a small, square house in the heart of the township. It was here that we would be served dinner. As the students unloaded the bus, barefoot children from the neighborhood ran to greet us with radiant smiles and laughter. My students introduced themselves with hugs and handshakes until Arthur escorted us into the makeshift restaurant.

Once inside, the aroma of curried chicken, rice, vegetables, and spices filled the air. We walked through the kitchen and saw massive pots simmering on the stove. Bowls filled with vegetables of every color lined the counters. Our mouths watered in anticipation. We were led to a patio with long tables, ceiling fans, and African artwork. We bounced to the beat of djembe drums as we took our seats.

Arthur had arranged for some local students to join us for our feast, and as they filled in the seats among us, they told us about their lives, their township, their schools, and their hopes and dreams for the future. They lived in abject poverty, yet every student spoke three languages fluently—Xhosa, Zulu, and English. Some also knew how to speak in Afrikaans. Their ability to shift from one language to the next amazed and humbled us. When our students would ask the African students what they hoped to do in the future, the harsh realities of the remnants of apartheid surfaced. These students had no money for university and no way to earn or borrow it, either. They shared the same dreams that children all over the world have: to be doctors, business leaders, scientists, performers—their list was impressive. But no matter how hard they work, no matter how resilient or how persistent or even how hopeful, they have fewer realistic options. But it didn't seem to break their spirits. In fact, their spirits warmed our souls.

After our abundant feast, the tables were moved back, the stereo was turned up, and the little children from the township came running to the edge of the patio to join us for what was obviously routine: it was time to dance. And dance we did. Our students, our chaperones, the children of Soweto, the restaurant workers—we all laughed and sang and danced together. I looked over to see my students Osei and Ajee teaching steps to the smaller children who had gathered around them eager to attempt "American dance moves." Our students then learned the moves of the South Africans, and I climbed on top of a chair just to get the full view of the celebration unfolding before me. The experience was one of the most beautiful, uplifting moments of my entire life.

On the last night of the trip, we had the incredible opportunity to go to Pilanesberg National Park. We arrived at night, and as we departed the buses, Sydnei exclaimed, "Look up!" And there in the sky were the most vibrant stars I had ever seen. Excited to spend more time outside, we hurriedly checked in and then gathered on the lawn behind the hotel to lie on the soft grass and look up at the stars. They shone so brightly, and they seemed to go on forever—it was as if we had a view of the entire universe all at once. No one said a word as we lay there, heads and hands touching, just basking in the glory of the African night sky.

At last, Ahjanae and Dasia started to talk about how blessed they were just to be there, and how fortunate they realized they were after spending time with so many who had struggled so much. Alex and A'Lyric agreed, and then others joined in to talk about what things had deeply affected them—from the lack of food and shelter to how thankful the South African students seemed to be just to have a school at all. Jalen, Jule, and Zharia shared how much they enjoyed playing with the babies at the orphanage, and Jai, Osei, and Ajee loved dancing with the young children in the streets of Soweto. No one dared speak above a whisper, for it felt like we were lying there on sacred ground beneath the heavens, giving thanks for the opportunity and the appreciation that it instilled in each of us.

I was exhausted by the time I went to bed that night. But I giggled through tears as a spirit of gratitude filled me. I was thankful for so many things, and seeing it all through the eyes of my students had made it even more powerful. We had spent the night sitting still and appreciating God's majesty and the blessings that we had been given, as well as the joy of one another's company. It would have been easy to tell the kids to go to bed right when we'd arrived at the hotel after our long journey, but taking the time to give thanks increased the depth of our understanding tenfold.

When we give thanks for our many blessings, the trivial inconveniences and the trials of life are greatly diminished. When things don't go just as you expected and you don't get just what you want, give thanks anyway. I have even found that when life-changing moments happen, it is usually because there was a struggle beforehand that led to the joy of the experience. In fact, whenever we have lots of stress at work, our office manager, Mrs. Mosley, says it is because Satan is at work—he is not happy because he knows that we are on the verge of a huge blessing!

That group of students from that first trip to South Africa continues to be a big part of my life, even though they graduated several years ago. So when Dasia had her latest big idea, I readily went along with it.

"Oooo! Mrs. Bearden! Why don't all of the 2010 girls have another slumber party . . . but this time, let's have it in the school!"

"Hmmm . . . I guess that we could. No one has ever done that before. Why not?" I said.

"Can we do it over Thanksgiving break?" she asked.

I just couldn't say no. Since our graduates are scattered at different high schools all over the country, it is always wonderful to spend time with them all together. On the night of the big sleepover, Ron, my husband, Scotty, and the boys from their class joined us for dinner, and then afterward we had a grand time playing hide-and-seek in the building with all the lights out. We played Nerf ball wars, too, and we chased each other up and down the halls, shrieking with laughter.

Once the boys left, we put on our pajamas, moved the desks in my room to the side, and surrounded ourselves with pillows, blankets, potato chips, and cookies. Aujahuna appointed herself as the DJ, and she put on one fun song after another. The girls danced, giggled, and talked about everything . . . high school triumphs and challenges, cool clothes, and of course, cute boys.

Then Dasia had another idea: "Let's go to every room in the school and talk about our favorite memory that happened in each one."

Alex said, "What about the ghosts?" Since our school has, at times, had many unexplained noises, I humored this worry and downloaded the Ghost-o-meter app on my phone to help us hunt them down. Arm in arm, we shuffled about in our jammies and stocking feet, stopping in each darkened room to relive our time together. We squealed and darted out of the old detention hall room when the Ghost-o-meter went haywire. We recounted the year that Mr. Clark had built the "gauntlet"—a full-sized academic obstacle course—in another room. The girls remembered tears and laughter. They recalled poignant lessons, memorable interactions with their teachers, who had liked whom and other relationship drama, and how close they had been. And as they shared their precious memories with me, I was filled with joy and appreciation.

When we collapsed back in my room, Ahjanae said, "What we have is special. When I try to explain it to my high school friends, they just don't get it."

"I knoooowww!" said ChiChi. "When I told people that I was having a slumber party with my middle school friends and my middle school teacher at our school, well . . . they thought it was weird!"

"I know, right?!" said Ahjanae. "We are so blessed."

Alex added, "Yeah, people don't know what it is like to have friendships like ours."

"And teachers like ours . . . We are so lucky to have teachers who will love all of us forever," said Aujahuna.

"We are family," said Zharia. "No matter what, we are family."

The warmth of the experience enveloped me as I drifted off to the sounds of their giggles. Later, I woke to find that all the girls had finally dozed off. As I thought back on our time together, I couldn't fall back asleep so I decided to walk around the school again, reflecting on my own.

I stopped when I got to the grand staircase in the heart of the school. Looking up at the stars filtering through the skylight, I sat down on the landing. And there, I relived five and a half years of precious memories. I was by myself, but I did not feel alone. As I reminisced, I saw the faces of our children laughing and cheering in the lobby, and I heard their voices and their singing. I thought about my family, who had supported me in creating this school, and every adult who has worked with our students, and I gave thanks for each one. I prayed for the families of our students and for every teacher who had visited our school and the students whom they affect. I prayed for every child I've taught and those I have yet to teach. And all the while, tears of gratitude streamed down my face.

And then an even stronger sense of appreciation filled me as I gave thanks for the challenges I had faced in my life. I was overcome with peace as I realized that by experiencing pain I had taught myself the power of joy; enduring betrayal had taught me the importance of loyalty and forgiveness; feeling hopeless had taught me the power of faith; and being hurt by another had taught me the need to uplift and love others. Living with financial hardship had taught me to value what really matters and to help those in need, and feeling insignificant had taught me to find my voice.

By seeing the world through the eyes of children, I have learned the abounding power of love, joy, and laughter. They have taught me that deep inside, I have the strength to choose how to live my life . . . and I choose a life with purpose, passion, and appreciation. Fellowship, love, music, laughter—they are available to us all.

As the purple haze of morning began to filter through the night sky, I returned to my pillow, smiling. I fell asleep, excited about the limitless possibilities of the day that lay ahead. No matter where my path would lead me next, I planned to appreciate the journey.

And I hope that you will do the same.

CRASH COURSE

- CLASS NOTES -

- Realize that our worth is not measured by what we own; rather, it is measured by who we are.
- It is okay to have nice things, but not at the expense of good relationships.
- Learn to distinguish between what you need and what you want; don't confuse the two.
- Children need our love and our time more than they need material possessions.
- The constant pursuit of materialism drains us and leaves us less able to enjoy what truly matters.
- Love, laughter, fellowship—these are the kinds of things that matter the most.

- HOMEWORK -

I. Ask your child to make a list of the things that he or she would really like to have from you. Tell them that the list cannot contain anything that costs money. Sit down together and discuss ways to strengthen your relationship based on things that matter to you both.

2. Make a list of the things that make you a person of worth. Now go back through that list and cross out the things that are tied to your material possessions or success. What is left?

3. Keep a journal of your top memories. Notice what makes those memories significant.

4. Keep a record of how you spend your spare time. Whatever takes up the most space should be what matters the most to you.

5. Learn to write down the things for which you are grateful each day, even when you are struggling with life's challenges.

6. Take the time to show appreciation to those around you. Write a note to someone just to let them know that you are grateful for your relationship with them and for their friendship or support.

7. Instill a spirit of appreciation in your children. Teach them how to show appreciation in word and in deed.

17

FAITH

================ COURSE DESCRIPTION ================

In this class, you will learn how children offer a glimpse into the
nature of God.

As our tour bus pulled up in front of the historic Abyssinian
Baptist Church on our field trip to Harlem, New York, we had
no idea what awaited us. My students, the other chaperones,
and I filed into the church pews, surprised to see that the
venue was already packed with visitors. Both the day and the
church were cold and damp, and we huddled together as we
waited for what had been billed as the Hour of Power.

Organ music suddenly swelled from the pulpit as one of the
reverends walked out to greet all who were there. As he con-
versed with the congregants, we were amazed to hear that the

audience contained guests from Sweden, Germany, England, Ghana, Korea, and other countries around the globe. Still others came from states all across America. It seemed that the whole world was represented in that small space.

The choir entered and took their places. As the organ music crescendoed, their angelic voices echoed throughout the sanctuary. This ARC Gospel Choir was no ordinary choir; *ARC* stands for Addicts Rehabilitation Center, and after they sang, the members shared stories about their personal struggles, about faith, about healing, and about salvation. These performers sang with pain, with compassion, and a spirit of redemption that filled the room with joy.

When they burst into "Oh Happy Day," Devin could no longer contain himself. He jumped from his seat and moved into the aisle, clapping and singing at the top of his lungs. And then, one at a time, I watched my students—of all faiths—do the same thing. They were all completely caught up in the joy of "Oh Happy Day." It seemed as if God's very presence had permeated every inch of that room and had showered happiness over all of us. We were bound together in this moment, and when God's presence hasn't seemed nearly as tangible or near, I have often thought back on that day.

This book is written for people who have varying faiths or who have no faith at all, but since it comes from my heart, it would be impossible not to share my thoughts on my faith with you. My faith has, after all, been the foundation for the path that I have taken—it is my core, and it is woven into all of the lessons I share with you. It is the lens through which I view my world. I believe that each of us is born with a void that is designed to be filled. Many people spend their lives trying to fill this space with the wrong things—money, material possessions, drugs, alcohol, fame, relationships, food, work, thrill seeking—and while some of these things might bring temporary happiness, they alone are not enough to lead to fulfillment.

I have known many people who have made great achievements, have special talents, and own extravagant possessions, yet many of them find that there's still something missing. The individuals that I know who have *it*—consistent joy, peace, happiness, and fulfillment despite life's circumstances—have one common denominator: an unwavering, true relationship with the Creator; they have a faith that guides them and sustains them. And they understand that there is a difference between religion and faith. One can have religion—a set of behaviors around a prescribed doctrine—but lack an understanding of what it is to truly believe and trust in God.

I felt the presence of God that day in Harlem, but there have been other times when He felt far, far away. I have learned that faith is more than just a feeling.

On that class trip to South Africa, we visited orphanages in addition to the schools. When we entered the first orphanage, we were greeted by a jolly, kind woman who had far more children than she could possibly tend to with her limited staff. Cribs filled every inch of the room. The lighting was poor, but the orphanage was clean, and the pungent smell of disinfectant saturated the air. As my students approached the cribs, the toddlers all leapt to their feet with arms outstretched. Without hesitation, my students began picking them up and playing with them. The room was filled with laughter as I watched my eighth-grade boys tenderly playing with children who climbed all over them. The girls, too, started to soothe and rock the children, and I was taken aback by how every single one of my students readily embraced those orphans. Some began feeding them oatmeal at the caretaker's urging, and others even took on changing diapers. Not one single student showed fear or reluctance; they showered those little children with pure love and affection.

It was all too much. A huge lump formed in my throat, and I felt my eyes filling with tears. I knew that I couldn't break down in front of the kids, so I quietly left the room and went out to the back of the building. It was there that I dropped to my knees and began to sob. Suddenly I felt someone's hand on my back. I was gently lifted up by the elbows, turned around, and hugged as I heard the words "I know. It's okay. It's okay."

You see, Hakeem, an eighth-grade student, had noticed me leave with tears in my eyes, and he followed me, just to make sure I was okay. A strong, bright young man, Hakeem was known for being the class clown, not the comforter. Sometimes he was the tough guy; sometimes he was even disruptive. But in that moment, he showed great compassion and kindness, and I was able to see a glimpse into the man that I knew he could become. I imagined him comforting a little girl of his own one day, and my heart was filled with hope—both for his future, and the future of our world.

I would later cling to that hope after Hakeem graduated. Of all of our graduates, he was the one who really struggled after leaving RCA. He was having so much fun in high school that he got into trouble with his grades and with some unseemly friends. He withdrew from all of us who tried to check up on him, and he struggled in many other ways. He lived with a twenty-two-year-old aunt, and he made poor choices—really poor ones. Hakeem was eventually sent away to a military-type boarding school, where he did receive his GED, but when he returned to his old friends, the old behaviors came back as well.

Each night I would pray for Hakeem, but my faith would falter as I wondered if we had lost him. Our staff members prayed for him, too. But faith requires both prayer and stepping out to take action. The men of RCA, including some of our wonderful dads, came up with a game plan: They would all take turns calling Hakeem, mentoring him, and taking him to dinner. They would refuse to allow him to push them away—he would have no choice but to understand that we all loved him and that no matter what he did, it would not change that. We would love him unconditionally, just as God loves us all.

And so Hakeem was offered a job at RCA, helping with our lunch program. And every day when he walks through our doors and flashes his beautiful smile, I am reminded of God's presence and faithfulness. The void in Hakeem's life was filled with our love and prayers. The young man whom I witnessed in South Africa has returned to us, and this winter, he started college. This summer, he will begin serving our country as a proud member of the United States Navy.

When educators attend training at RCA, they spend the day in our classrooms getting to know our amazing students. When teachers recount their favorite parts of the visit, they inevitably mention our students' warmth, joy, kindness, and enthusiasm. And so when it is time to conclude the day, we want our visitors to take that joy with them.

After these guests finish the day and are "slide certified"—an RCA tradition where they slide down our two-story tube slide for the very first time—the entire student body joins them in the lobby and sings a very special song to them. Our students surround the guests and hold their hands as they sing how they believe in them as teachers and that they are appreciated. Many adults cry at this point. My dear friend Holly, a wonderful counselor, cried and cried on one such day—so much so that she could hardly control her sobs. When I asked her why she was so overcome, she responded, "Everywhere I looked, there were beautiful children of all different colors with radiant faces just singing so joyfully. I was certain in that moment that it was exactly what heaven must feel like."

If you need to develop a deeper understanding of faith, spend time with children. Watch how they love without reservation, how they believe what you promise, and how they look forward to each and every day. Children's hearts are a perfect reminder of the pure goodness that awaits us in heaven. By devoting my life to them, I have been blessed to experience a slice of heaven while still here on earth.

And that is the greatest lesson of all.

CLASS NOTES

- We are born with a void that is meant to be filled.
- Many individuals spend their lives trying to fill this void with unhealthy things.
- Religion and faith can be two different things.
- Faith is more than just a feeling.
- When we stumble, we learn the true meaning of faith and hope.
- God's presence is all around us—we just have to notice.
- Children's hearts give us a window to God.

HOMEWORK

1. Make a list of the things that you use to fill the voids in your life. Note the things that are negatively affecting your faith. How can you replace these things with more spirituality?

2. Seek to understand your current belief system. If you feel that you need more spirituality in your life, set out to find answers. If you doubt, remember that some individuals with the deepest faith are those who once doubted and asked the most questions!

3. Consider adding frequent prayer to your life if you do not already do so. Don't know what to say? Just speak from the heart. God is moved by your heart, not the words you choose.

4. Look for evidence of God's majesty all around you. Record the blessings you see in a journal.

5. Spend time with children, and focus on their pure, loving spirits.

ABOUT THE
RON CLARK ACADEMY

The Ron Clark Academy is a highly acclaimed, nonprofit middle school in Atlanta that promotes innovation and engages its students through energetic teaching balanced by a strict code of discipline. Each year, thousands of educators from around the world participate in RCA's professional development training to learn how to replicate the school's style, philosophy, and success in their own schools.

While at RCA, participants have the opportunity to observe four to five highly acclaimed master teachers instructing classes of children with various levels of academic, social, and emotional development. In addition to the classroom observations, educators also attend three to four workshops throughout the course of the day. A focus is placed on showing educators how to increase student engagement, promote academic rigor, and create a climate and culture for student success.

To learn more about the RCA's staff development programs, please visit www.ronclarkacademy.com.

ACKNOWLEDGMENTS

To my dear husband, Scotty: My depth of love for you is endless. Thank you for loving me, supporting me, understanding me, and being my rock. I am so blessed to be your wife.

To my precious Madison: You are my heart and my joy. I am so honored to be your mim, and I am so very proud of you. The world has yet to see all that you can do—you are destined for greatness!

To Richard Abate: I would like to thank you for being a wonderful agent and for being the first to believe in my vision for a book. You have guided and supported me from the beginning, and this book would not have happened without you.

To Priscilla Painton: Priscilla, the best teachers push, support, encourage, and set the highest of expectations. Turns out you have been far more than my editor; you have been one of the best teachers that I have ever had. Thank you for

ACKNOWLEDGMENTS

challenging me to discover what truly defines my work as an educator. I am forever grateful.

To Sydney Tanigawa: Thank you for also being an incredible editor and for being so responsive and helpful whenever I had a need or a question. I appreciate you!

To Duane Ward, Ryan Giffen, and the rest of the team at Premiere Speakers Bureau: It has been an honor to be represented by you for the past fourteen years. Thank you for providing me with the privilege to speak to thousands of educators across this country and around the world. I greatly appreciate all that you have done for RCA and for me.

To my parents: I love you both so very much, and I am so blessed to have you in my life. You always believed in me, and you taught me the power of unconditional love. Because of you, I knew that I could become anything that my heart desired.

To my brothers, Bobby and Stephen: Thank you for teaching me how to be strong, courageous, and resilient. You showed me how to laugh at myself, and with you protecting me, I always knew that everything would be okay.

To the Supper Club—Linda, Rhonda, Beth, and Jennifer: Thank you for twenty years of beautiful friendship. The laughter, love, support, and memories have given me such joy.

ACKNOWLEDGMENTS

To Ed, Holly, Kevin, Beth, Scott, Donna, David, Michelle, Blake, and Shelly: I cherish our vacations and times spent together. Thank you for being such a special, wonderful part of my life and for continuously encouraging me throughout the writing of this book.

To J. W.: Thank you for thirty-seven years of friendship and laughter.

To Michelle Lambert: Thank you for listening and for helping Madison and me pick up the pieces. You forever changed our lives.

To the Marus Family: This book was sparked by our front porch talks and your continuous support throughout the years. I love you all so very much.

To Mona Hurley: You exemplify the woman that I hope to become. I know that God had a very specific plan when he placed you in my life, and I am forever grateful for your love and guidance.

To Kyle Unglaub: Thank you for the gift you gave to me. Whenever I think of our time together, I smile.

To Steven and Jill Butler: Thank you for always being there for Madison and me. Your support and friendship mean so much to us.

ACKNOWLEDGMENTS

To J. Amezqua: Thank you for capturing the images of our precious students and for being such a wonderful role model. Your photography skills are extraordinary, and RCA considers you to be one of our greatest gifts.

To my former coworkers in Cobb County Schools: Thank you for teaching me, nurturing me, guiding me, supporting me, and molding me into the teacher that I am today. It was your talent that inspired me to do more, be more, and become more.

To the board of the Ron Clark Academy: Your commitment to our children is unparalleled. I deeply appreciate the countless hours and incredible support that you give to us all. Because of your efforts, we are able to continue to thrive.

To our sponsors: RCA is truly blessed by your resources, time, and talents. Because of you, we are able to affect the lives of students around the world.

To the parents of my students, past and present: Thank you for giving me the privilege to teach, grow with, and love your children. I have learned so much from your support, your parenting, and your love.

To the staff of the Ron Clark Academy: You are the hardest-working, most extraordinary people I know. Thank you for your joy, your passion, your brilliance, and your commitment to our children. You are my family, and I love you all so very much.

ACKNOWLEDGMENTS

To my students, past and present: My world is brighter because you have been in it. This entire book was written to show my love and appreciation for you and the significant impact that you have had upon my life.

And to Ron Clark: Because I knew you . . .

About the Author

Kim Bearden is the cofounder, executive director, and language arts teacher at the Ron Clark Academy, an innovative middle school and educator training facility in Atlanta. Bearden has received numerous awards for her creative and dynamic teaching style, including the Disney American Teacher Awards Outstanding Middle School Humanities Teacher and the Milken Family Foundation Award for Excellence in Education. She is also a keynote speaker with Premiere Speakers Bureau, and each year she delivers messages to thousands of educators across the country and around the world to inspire them and teach them methods for engaging and motivating students.

Kim resides in Atlanta with her husband, Scotty, and daughter, Madison.